DR K[...]

Born in Solihull in 1945, Ki[...] [...] [...] the University of York whe[...] [...], Philosophy and Sociology and was later awarded a research fellowship. His Ph.D thesis 'Class Mobility in the Sixties' was published by Routledge and Kegan Paul in 1971. In 1973 he became a lecturer at Warwick University and in 1975 was appointed Reader in Demographics. Following a brief spell as Visiting Professor in Social Studies at Cornell University, he is now developing a major new Channel 4 series entitled 'Classwatching'.

SELINA FITZHERBERT

Born in Somerset in 1951, Selina Fitzherbert was educated in London, Switzerland, Italy and Paris, where her studies in the History of Fashion Design were interrupted when Roman Polanski discovered her in a school production of 'Romeo and Juliet'. During the late seventies, she appeared in 'Rutland Weekend Television', 'The Life Of Brian' and several episodes of 'The Professionals'. She is also a writer and photographer and has contributed articles on the social scene to *Ritz*, *Tatler* and *Harper's and Queen*. In partnership with Jaimie Belville, she will shortly be opening Buster, a contemporary design studio in the Fulham Road.

JEAN-LUC LEGRIS

Born in Paris in 1935, the son of Jean-Jacques Legris, France's leading translator of Shakespeare and Ben Jonson, M. Legris was evacuated in 1939 to Britain, where he was raised and educated. On returning to Paris, he set up an international marketing group and now advises companies throughout the world on image and product presentation. He is married to Suki Yarde-Buller, the celebrated restaurant critic, and their son Ned is currently at Eton.

THE COMPLETE NAFF GUIDE

Dr Kit Bryson, Selina Fitzherbert
and Jean-Luc Legris

Illustrations by Mark Reddy

Arrow Books

Arrow Books Limited
17-21 Conway Street, London W1P 6JD

An imprint of the Hutchinson Publishing Group

London Melbourne Sydney Auckland
Johannesburg and agencies throughout
the world

First published 1983
Reprinted 1983 (twice)

Set in Linotron Bembo by
Rowland Phototypesetting Limited
Bury St Edmunds, Suffolk

Made and printed in Great Britain
by The Guernsey Press Co Ltd
Guernsey, Channel Islands

ISBN 0 09 931760 5

CONTENTS

INTRODUCTION

With the gloves off in Mrs Thatcher's Britain, with mean-minded egalitarians in retreat and the stage-army of compassion lobbyists routed, it is, paradoxically (though not in any formal sense, of course), more important than ever to learn to box clever.

Would Mrs Thatcher herself be where she is today if she still looked, talked and acted like the daughter of a provincial grocer? The answer must be yes, because she does. But that is neither here nor there. She's got guts.

For the ordinary person with healthy social ambitions, it is precisely when the old rules no longer apply that a grasp of the rules is most essential. Didn't old Bill Shakespeare say:

'Take but degree away, untune that string
And hark what discord follows'?

Wise words indeed. Though we live in a time of social discord, or at least flux, this book is no mere guide to the present hierarchy, and how to disguise your derisory origins in it. Nor is it simply an advice manual on dress, accent and manners. Manners are important, of course. Didn't Wittgenstein say: 'Morals are etiquette'? In fact, he didn't. He said: 'Ethics are aesthetics', but the point holds. Manners oil the wheels of social intercourse and make it possible for us to live with one another. But with the resolute option in the driving seat and pragmatism off the leash, toes are there to be trodden on. Who, after all, won the mile in Moscow? Mr Nice-Guy, the mild-mannered Sebastian Coe or the abrasive, spiky Steve Ovett? Seb Coe, in fact, but he did it his way. He's got style.

To be naff is to be unstylish, whatever that may mean.

While the present authors cannot claim a comprehensive overview of what are the correct manners, opinions and modes of conduct in contemporary Britain, they do suggest that once you have read *The Complete Naff Guide* you will never again say the wrong thing in the wrong accent in the wrong place wearing the wrong clothes to the wrong person at the wrong time of day.

And who won the half-mile?

K.B.
S.T.F.A.F.
J-L. L.
London and Paris, 1983.

1
THE SOCIAL
FABRIC

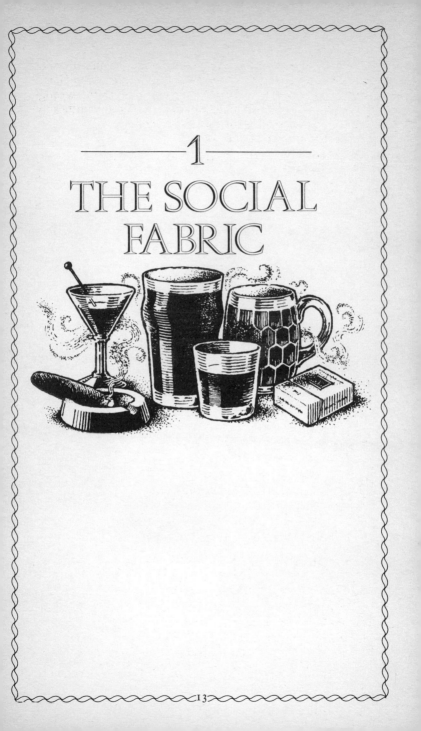

NAFF ACCENTS

North Circular (see Annie Walker and Mary
Whitehouse)

Aspiring upper–middle–class (see Liz Brewer)

Aspiring middle–class (see Lord Matthews)

Aspiring upper–lower–class (see Peter Cook)

The can't help it upper–class warble (see Lady Olga
Maitland)

The not–all–there mid–Atlantic (see David Frost)

The nothing–there–at–all disc–jockey, sport
commentator, media screech–speak (see David
Coleman, John Motson etc)

Dead common, one of the boys (see Maureen Lipman
and *Naff Actresses*)

Tetchy theatrical pansy (see Bill Gaskell)

White Rhodesian

Belfast

Birmingham

Janet Street–Porter

Canadian

NAFF WORDS

Naff
Brill
Pardon
Royals
Toilet
Blowjob
Boobs
Pantyhose
Trendy
Telly
Spondulicks
Serviette
Prang
Cheerio!

Irreverent
Celebrity
Hopefully
Viable
Options
Valid
Stylish
Wisecrack
Gag
Raconteur
Anecdote
Cerebral
Cruet
Beaver

NAFF WORDS

Underpants
Natch!
Charming!
Unisex
Pillock
Snobby
Kids
Parenting
Elitist
Quiche
Tits
Fellate
Costume
Kinky
Wacky
Hilarious
Sit-upon
Bonking
Boring
Pseudo

Wet
Zany
Shekels
Miz
Condiments
Freebie
Agreeable
Scrubber
Slag
Piles
Belly
Tinkle
Touché!
Womaniser
(see *Naff ex-Womanisers*)

Philosophy –
except to describe
what professional
philosphers do

Wank

NAFF EXPRESSIONS

Getting your leg over
Getting a bit
A bit of the other
A bit on the side
That can't be bad (see *Naff Barry Norman remarks*)
Pleased to meet you
Have a jar
Take a pew
Crack a gag
What's your poison?
Mine's a double
And I quote
Yours truly
Can I have hush?

My treat
It's open house
Help yourself right liberally
A nice drop of wine
This is it, this is it
Good in the sack
Thinking man's crumpet
I'm a tit–man myself
Pardon my French
My shout
Down the hatch
The little girl's room
The smallest room
Vital statistics
Look after number one
Rubber johnnies
At least it's a free meal
Mine host
Don't mind if I do
No sweat
Your place or mine?
Decisions, decisions!
Pork sword
Fairy ring
Beef bayonet
Buttered bun
Extract the digit
Horizontal jogging (see Max Hastings)
Golden shower
Water sports
Over the top
Come
Well I never did!
On your bike (see *Naff Politicians*)
Verbal diarrhoea
The lady wife
All part of the service
I should cocoa

NAFF EXPRESSIONS

Number One Son
Number Two Son
Senior citizen
Snuffing it
Some you win, some you lose (see *Naff Barry Norman remarks*)
Waxing philosophical
My kingdom for a horse!
Laugh? I thought they'd never dry!

NAFF AMERICAN EXPRESSIONS

Give head
Time frame
Do you know Jesus?
Buzz
Trip
Space
Coming from
Far out
I hear what you're saying
We can work something out between us, babe
Loosen up and have a line
Come by the house sometime
Like nowheresville
Like deadsville
Heavy bread
She couldn't get arrested in Rome (paradoxically, it's not naff really to get arrested in Rome)
It's in the can (not naff if you really are in the can)
Bankable
Kiss off (see *Naff Kiss-off Present*)
Go for it!

NAFF CHRISTIAN NAMES

Arnold	Nigel
Tina	Arthur

NAFF SURNAMES

Overy	Rummage
Biggs	Grobbelaar (see
Winkle	*Naff Goalkeepers*)
Bumstead	Humpage
Smith	Bourgois
Atkinson–Smythe	Brocklebank-Fowler
Davidson	Pygge
Patel	Penice
Powell	Vile
(but only when	Hawk
rhymed with bowel)	Shite
Pile	Jones
Foot	Beasley
Corn	Blunt
Belding	Clapp
Gobble	Norris
Fink	Phillips
Smellie	Blackhead
Snodgrass	Matthews
Nutter	Hoop
Brown	Rattle
Stubbs	Proops
Nobbs	Butt

2
THE HOME FRONT

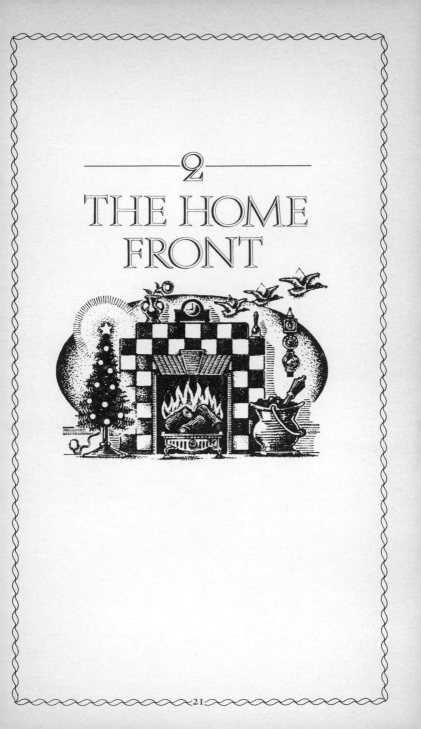

NAFF CLOTHING

Crocheted waistcoats
Sling-black shoes
Tuf shoes for men
Brown suits
Wide lapels
Donkey jackets
Anoraks with fur-lined
hoods
Nylon shirts
Vests
Paisley Y-fronts
Paisley ties (except
shooting)
Lycra figure-hugging
trousers (not to be confused
with stretch jeans)
Zip-boots (male or female)
Platform shoes
Cravats
See-through lace blouses
Boob tubes
Blazers with gold buttons
(not naff with Army or
Navy buttons)
Button-down collars
Checked jackets
Driving gloves
Flared jeans or trousers
Housecoats
Heeled fluffy slippers
Concertina granny
waterproof hoods
Chiffon square scarves
Child's two-piece bikini
Crimplene trousers
Stay-press trousers
Socks with open-toe
sandals

NAFF CLOTHING

Ankle socks folded over
Russian fur hats
Leopard-skin underwear
Nylon socks
Thermal underwear
String vests
Mittens
Medals
Shiny brown trousers
MCC tie except at Lords
Any shoes that need a
prescription
Battle fatigues
Shoulder-patched military
sweaters from Milletts
Berets
Reefer jackets
Gannex macs
Surgical stockings
Pre-tied bow ties
Cummerbunds
Pink dress shirts
Sweatshirts with
advertising legends
University scarves
Hush Puppies with a suit

NAFF HAT WEARERS

Sir Richard Attenborough
Gertrude Shilling
Quentin Crisp
Elton John
Orson Welles
Oddjob

Tommy Trinder
Brough Scott
David Coleman
Lindsay Anderson
Robin Hood
Mrs Thatcher
Huggy Bear
The bald Bee Gee

NAFF ACCESSORIES

HIM

Chain bracelets (esp.
identity bracelets)
Any rings except signet
rings
Purse for loose change
Medallions
Digital watches
Pocket calculators
Onyx cuff-links
Tie-pins
Monocles
Leather-studded wrist
bands
Dark-glasses indoors
(unless member of secret
police)
Swordsticks
Initials on shirts,
dressing-gowns, etc.
Roses sewn on to disco
pumps, handbags etc.

HER

Crucifix dangle earrings
Large fake single stone
rings
Poppet pearls

NAFF ACCESSORIES

Anklets
Slave bracelets
Charm bracelets
Winged glasses
Spectacle chain
Initials on handbags
Poodles
Toyboys
Walkers (see *Naff Walkers*)

NAFF WALKERS

Norman Lonsdale
Ned Ryan
Derek Deane
Gayelord Hauser (walked
for Garbo)
Jerry Zipkin
The Walker Brothers
Nancy Walker (see *Naff
Nancies*)

NAFF PLACES TO
LIVE

St John's Wood
Surrey
Essex
Mayfair
Cheam
Sunningdale
Kingston

Barnes
Putney
Chiswick
Guildford
Weybridge
Chobham
Jersey
Canada

NAFF NAMES FOR
HOUSES

The Gables
Squirrels' Nest
Dunroamin'
The Larches
The Firs
Chez Nous
Mon Repos
My Folly!
Truncheons (see *Naff Judges*)
The Moorings
Any combination of the owners' names or parts thereof:
eg. Desther or Anthebruce (see *Naff Couples*)
Sea View
Bella Vista
Calling your house a Court if it isn't
My Way
Honeysuckle Cottage
'The Gasworks' – for the House of Commons
It is extremely naff to have the name of your house
engraved on a piece of wood on the front gate

NAFF HOUSEHOLD OBJECTS

NAFF SITTING-ROOM OBJECTS

Net curtains
Stereo or TV in teak finish
Crouching Atlas holding TV on back
Teak coffee tables
A copy of *Goodbye Baby And Amen* by David Bailey and
Peter Evans on glass-topped coffee-table from
Peter Jones
Three-piece suites
Poofs
Fake leather furniture
Fab fur cushions with one button in the middle
Bars
Wall heaters
Red tiled fireplaces
Coal tidies
Flowered wall-to-wall carpets
Antimacassars
Fire gloves
Fab fur fireside rugs
Glass hand-bell for summoning servants
White wedding photograph album
Silver plastic Christmas trees with fairy lights
Bead curtains
Brass and glass furniture
Trompe l'œil of Mediterranean views
Graduated ducks
Oil blooping lamps
Posters, esp. Warhol's 'Monroe'
Prints, esp. 'The Tahitian Girl', Van Gogh's
'Sunflowers', Constable's 'Haywain'
Photographs of self with celebrities
Gaslog fires
Sporting trophies in cabinet
Aquarium
Horse brasses
Children

Dogs
Cocktail cabinets
Light dimmers
Light machines
Blow heaters
Plastic holder for records
Dummy books
Souvenir ashtrays, esp. from Toledo
Marble eggs
Onyx anything
Squatters

NAFF DINING-ROOM OBJECTS

Fish knives
Cruet sets (salt, pepper, vinegar and mustard trays)
Oil and vinegar set in raffia basket
Steak knives
Serviette rings

NAFF THINGS TO FIND IN THE LAVATORY

Musical lavatory roll
Pedestal sets
Humorous lavatory paper, especially with crosswords
Coloured flush, esp. Brobat
Seat cosy
The *Tatler*
Erotic magazines, esp. *Penthouse*
Lilac deodorant spray
Humorous Christmas books, esp. by Frank Muir

NAFF BEDROOM OBJECTS

His and Her pillowcases
Fur-lined walls
Circular bed
Waterbed
Computerised bed
Teasmade clock radio
Vibrator

NAFF BEDROOM OBJECTS

Black sheets
Erotic pictures on walls (esp. nudes bought in
Bayswater Road on Sunday)
Rowing machine
Bullworker
Mirror on ceiling
Nylon sheets
Television
Video camera (esp. if concealed)
Wig
Dirty comb
Spilling ashtrays
Used cotton buds
Bondage attachments on bed-corners
Box of Kleenex near bed (unless in call-girl's flat)
Two-way mirror

NAFF THINGS TO FIND IN THE BATHROOM

Black bath with gold taps
His and Her towels
Towel stolen from Strand Palace Hotel
Flannels
Loofahs
Crystal tap handles
Shagpile carpet on floor
Linoleum on floor
Geoffrey Wheatcroft asleep on floor (see *Naff Hacks*)
Vista tiling
Mirror-tiles, bought at Peter Jones, for steamy
self-appraisal after bath
Erotica on walls
False teeth in glass
Pubic shavings in basin
Phallic soap
Lemon-scented soap
Avacado bathroom suites
Kidney-shaped baths
Bathmat with 'bathmat' written on it

NAFF THINGS TO FIND IN THE BATHROOM CABINET

Grecian 2000
Preparation 'H' suppositories
Corn-plasters
Liquid paraffin
Electric toothbrush
Listerine mouth-wash
Denture fixatives

NAFF KITCHEN OBJECTS

Comical aprons
Hen-shaped egg-holders
Fondue sets
Woks
Pressure cookers
Collection of Robert Carrier cookbooks
Noticeboard for silly messages from woman of house
to herself

NAFF THINGS TO FIND IN THE HALL

Umbrella stand made out of elephant's foot
Visitor's book
Welcome mat
Bicycles
Telephone
Childrens' toys, esp. roller-skates
Prams
Squash rackets or golf clubs

NAFF THINGS TO FIND IN THE GARDEN

Crazy paving
Rockery
Gnomes
Herbaceous borders
Fish ponds
Swing-seats
Patio
Gazebo
Conservatory

NAFF THINGS TO FIND IN THE GARDEN

Plastic swimming pool
Bird table
Privet hedge

NAFF SMELLS

Tweed
Brut
Boiled eggs
Firelighters
Wet dogs
Babies
Lungs
Ironing
Cooking popcorn
Wrens' barracks
Fringe theatres

3
THE ANIMAL KINGDOM

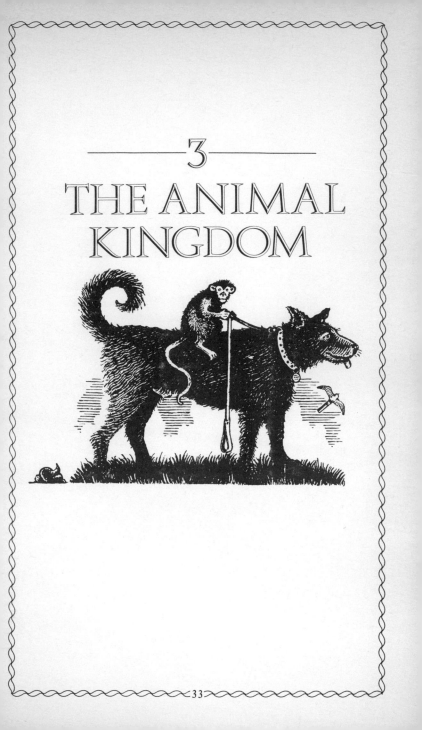

NAFF PETS

Pythons
Newts
Canaries
Budgerigars
Fish
Carnivorous plants (but not carnivorous fish)
Tortoises (paradoxically, not terrapins)
Ferrets
Mice
Hamsters
Gerbils
Fleas
Dwarves
Monkeys
Toads

NAFF DOGS

Dobermans
Alsatians
Chihuahuas
Poodles
Corgis
Fox Terriers
Pekinese
Great Danes
Coon hounds
Greyhounds (but not whippets)
Mastiffs
Sealyhams

NAFF NAMES FOR DOGS

Adolf
Hymie

NAFF NAMES FOR DOGS

Helga
Dolores
Rex

NAFF WAYS OF KILLING
YOUR NEIGHBOUR'S DOBERMAN

Mince

NAFF CATS

There are no naff cats, however it is extremely naff to
keep a leopard

NAFF THINGS TO TEACH
YOUR PARROT TO SAY

Evening all!
Fuck the Pope

NAFF FISH

Mackerel
Dogfish
Hake
Sole meunière

——4——
ON THE ROAD

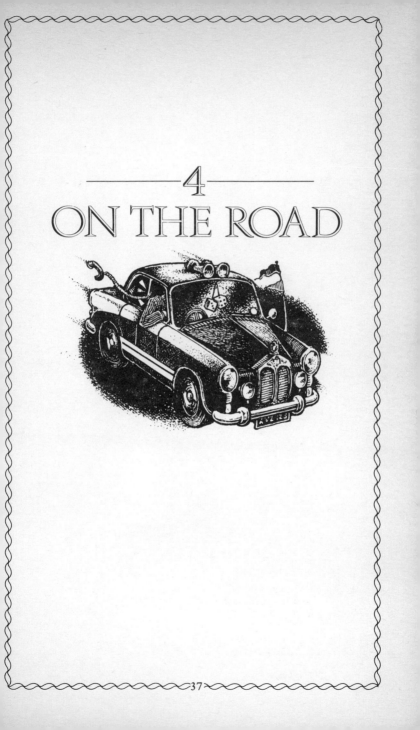

NAFF CARS

All Fords, Vauxhalls, Toyotas or Dafs
Renault 5 (but not 4)
Hillman Imp
Minx
Triumph Spitfire
Datsun 240Z
Gold Rolls Royce
Chocolate coloured Range Rover

NAFF CAR ACCESSORIES

National pennants or nodding dogs in rear window
Air ball freshener on rear window ledge
Fab fur fitted seat covers
Green stick–on visors on windscreen (esp. naff if they
incorporate the names of the owners)
Driving gloves
Magnetic mileage recorders
Drink cabinets
Two–tone horn
Bugle horn
Dice hanging from rear vision mirror
Car–tidy
Telephone
Steering wheel cosies
Roof–racks (should buy bigger car)
Rally spotlight
CB radio aerial
Bumper stickers (see *Naff Bumper Stickers*)

NAFF BUMPER STICKERS

I hate JR
My other car's a Porsche
My other car's a Mini

Nuke the whales
Re-elect Nicholas Scott MP
I've upped my income – Up Yours!
Warning! Mark Thatcher taught me to drive
Achilles is a heel
Nurses do it with patience
(Peter Grosvenor writes: 'Though the world may not
be your oyster every Cortina can be your canvas!' see
Naff Literary Editors)

NAFF DRIVING HABITS

Gunning engine in a jam
Stopping suddenly to talk to Sloanes
Curb-crawling
Squashing hedgehogs
Driving when too drunk to walk (see Mel Smith)
Devouring – with hysterical use of horn, lights –
underpowered cars in outside motorway lanes
Resting elbow through window, hand on roof
Beating steering wheel in time to music
Packing six shrieking under-twenty-one-year-olds in an
open car
Stop-starting a garbage truck at 5 a.m. in residential
street
Driving beyond your capacity to impress female
elements

5
THE PRIVATE
PERSON

NAFF PARTS OF THE BODY

Feet
Sinuses
Adenoids
Epiglottis
Scrotum
Men's nipples
Armpits
Nostrils

NAFF THINGS TO DO WITH PARTS OF THE BODY

Wink
Penetrate unexpectedly (see *Naff Sexual Practices*)
Snap fingers at waiters (see *Naff Things To Do In Restaurants*)
Squelch eyes with fingers
Circular OK signs
Thumbs up/down (unless at prep school)
Adjust lie of penis through trouser pocket
Worry spots
Pick teeth
Comb hair in public
Scratch crutch
Scratch colon
Hand-jive
Clench and unclench buttock-muscles when standing at bar in tightish trousers

NAFF PERSONAL HABITS AND BEHAVIOUR

Hang tights over bath
Attend voice-training class, unless actress (see Mrs Thatcher)

NAFF PERSONAL HABITS AND BEHAVIOUR

Pay bills on time

Not pay bills at all

Count your change in shops

Hit women

Wash feet in bidet

Share a bath

Watch blue films in company and offer humorous running–commentary involving jokes about eating celery

Live in an iron–lung

Sing along

Clear throat like a Greek

Tell jokes, esp. involving regional or foreign accents, esp. Indian

Cap stories

Converse in assumed accents (see Peter Cook)

Sell your memoirs to the *People* (see *Naff Newspapers*). Paradoxically it isn't naff to sell your memoirs to the *News Of The World* if (a) you're a woman, (b) you receive at least £100,000 and (c) you can mention a sexual involvement with at least one member, preferably male, of the Royal family. It is *always* naff for a man to sell his memoirs to the *News Of The World* unless he is a snooker player or football manager, and even then it's naff

Have an au pair

Belong to an indoor nudist club

Put in for a pay rise. Attractive and talented people simply change jobs (see Selina Scott)

Go carol singing

Stand as comical candidate at General Election (see William Rushton)

Submit anything to 'Pseuds Corner'. Paradoxically, it's not naff of them to publish it, since ageing minor public schoolboys cannot be expected to distinguish between the pretentious and the daring

Put an advertisement in *The Times* to say that you are not sending out Christmas cards this year but are instead giving the money to charity

Send Christmas cards showing photograph of self, family or house (see *Naff Things The Royal Family Do*)

Send out humorously worded invitation, designed by yourself, to a bottle-party celebrating your fortieth birthday

Be made redundant at forty-five

Inform on neighbour to Social Security watchdogs. It is even naffer to inform on defaulting tradesmen to consumer watchdogs in the media, esp. Esther Rantzen and her attendant half-wits (see *Naff Sneaks*)

Send your wife into a newsagent to buy *Gay News* while you hover outside

Take a day-trip to Boulogne to avail yourself of duty-free bargains

Send nude photograph of your wife to 'Readers' Wives' feature of *Knave* or *Fiesta*

Go to a tea-dance (see *Naff Things To Do After The Age Of Forty* and *Naff Old Romeos*)

Have a season ticket for Queens Park Rangers

Appear on a chat-show, esp. if you purport to be a serious person. Thus it is naff for Jonathan Miller to appear on 'The Parkinson Show', but not naff of Peter Cook to do so (see *Naff Members of 'Beyond The Fringe'*)

Be blackmailed by a male prostitute (see *Naff Things To Do After The Age of Forty*)

Introduce yourself unexpectedly into the Queen's bedroom

Send a present to the Royal family

Line the route waving a small Union Jack

Have your memoirs ghosted, esp. by Sharon Ring or Don Short

Go without holidays in order to educate your children privately (see *Naff Boasts*)

Bank with the TSB

Devise and appear in a one-man show

Quote whole scenes from 'Casablanca'

NAFF PERSONAL HABITS AND BEHAVIOUR

Quote poetry, except Eliot, Auden, Whitworth, Ewart, Larkin (*not* 'They fuck you up, your mum and dad') or at least twenty-five lines of Kipling

Be a Conservative intellectual. However, if you meet a Conservative intellectual it is extremely naff to say: 'A Conservative intellectual? Isn't that a contradiction in terms? Haw! Haw!'

Have your name printed on a bullfight poster between those of Paco Camino and El Cordobes

Put a humorous announcement on your answering-machine (see Peter Cook and *Naff Things Lonely People Do*)

Leave humorous messages on someone else's answering machine

Attend The Woman Of The Year Lunch

It's naff to appear nude in *Mayfair* or *Men Only*, but not *Playboy* or *Penthouse*

Collect humorous records, esp. by Peter Sellers, or quote from *National Lampoon* records

Publish a book of cute sayings by children

Write a non-book, esp. timed to catch the stocking-filler market

Write children's books, esp. if you're an ex-personality or a middle-aged actress (see *Naff Ex-Personalities* and Nanette Newman)

It's extremely naff of men to possess photographs of themselves unless they are actors or models, and even then it's naff

It's very naff, if you can't have children, to buy a dwarf in Turkey

Do your own conveyancing to save money

Mix up a punch in the bidet

Send a girlfriend a male singing strippergram on her birthday

Play practical jokes, esp. stretching cling-wrap over lavatory bowl

Watch breakfast TV

Appear on breakfast TV (see *Naff Couples*)

Sell an idea for a book to Lord Weidenfeld for a
vastly inflated sum and then not deliver (see Anna Ford)

NAFF THINGS TO BE

Stuffed up
Overtaken by events
Caught short
On parole
On bail
Redundant
A member of the general public
An ordinary mother
A man in the street
On your last legs
On the rebound
A rank-and-file member
An unsung hero
In analysis
Saving up for a rainy day
Eighty-three-years-young

NAFF PLACES TO BE

Between two stools
On a slippery slope
In a grey area
In the limelight (see *Naff Things The Royal Family Do*)
In no-man's land
Out on a limb
Down Your Way
Over the top
Over a barrel
At the end of your tether
On the spot
In the hot seat

In a total exclusion zone
In a recession
In the headlines
In a no-go area
On the horns of a dilemma
In snooker
In the spotlight
In the *News Of The World*
In the shit
In Belgium

NAFF THINGS TO BE AFRAID OF

HER
Italian drivers
Parrots
The cleaning lady
Going to parties
Black men
Looking available
What her mother might think
Being caught in her curlers
Being asked what her job is
Whether she can combine a career with being a good
mother
Whether she's a viable human being
Burning the food
That her guests will twig that the butterscotch dessert is
Bird's Instant Whip
That her bottom's too fat

HIM
That his bottom's too fat
That his guests will twig that the butterscotch dessert is
Bird's Instant Whip
Mice

Spiders
Women
Bank managers
Wine waiters
Appearing on television
Not appearing on television (see Clive James)

NAFF MENTAL AFFLICTIONS

Delusions of grandeur
Anything requiring electro-convulsive therapy
Anal retentive power worship (see Mrs Thatcher's
cocktail cabinet)
Stammering
Anorexia Nervosa
Asthma Nervosa
Compulsion to appear on television (see Clive James)
Compulsion to write batty letters to the *Daily Telegraph*

'Sir,
   The worst feature of Channel 4 is not the use of four-letter words but the quite appalling prospect that 1983 is to be heralded in with an entertainment for so-called gays. Perhaps we shall soon have Blunt *et al* in transvestite dance routines and Moscow phone-ins with the growing list of sexual deviant traitors.
   Compassion in the country for homosexuals and lesbians is in most cases a licence for permissiveness, perversion and decadence and is unceasingly exploited by the Russians who are only too well aware that twisted or twistable minds frequently go hand in hand with sexual perversion.
   It is no coincidence that the Gay Lib, CND and World Peace Movements are riddled with those to the far-left politically and sexual deviants. Many of those involved in these movements are the unwitting tools of the Russians as are a number of leftist deviants in the media.
   What we require now is not a rebuilding of a Political Warfare Service but a counter-subversion organisation. Such a department, without encroaching on freedom of speech and freedom of the press, could issue counter-subversive propaganda and through liaison with our security services covertly attempt to nip in the bud further communist-inspired efforts to undermine our society before they bear fruit.
Robin Bruce Lockhart, Hove, Sussex.'

NAFF PHYSICAL AFFLICTIONS

Eczma
Acne
Dandruff
Herpes
Sweating like a horse
Body odour – paradoxically, not halitosis, which shows
signs of strong character (see Michael Foot)
Verucas
Crabs
Incontinence
Catarrh
Cleft palette
Tatoos (see Paula Yates)

NAFF OPERATIONS

Tonsils (paradoxically not adenoids)
Vasectomy (see Michael Parkinson)
Varicose veins
Nose job (see Peter O'Toole)
Face-lifts (see Nancy Reagan. Every time she smiles she
pulls her knickers up)
Buttock-lifts (see Lord Bradwell. Every time he sat
down his hat fell off)
Haemmorhoids
Ingrowing toenails
Hair implants, esp. pubic
Sex change
Hernia
Removal of sweat glands
Attempted penis enlargement
Any silicone infusions
All teeth out
Transplanting toes on to hand to replace fingers
Draining sinuses

Syringing ears
Waxing legs (for men – see John Inman)
Operation Swamp (see *Naff Police Operations*)

NAFF CAUSES OF DEATH

Cirrhosis of liver
Motorway madness on M61
Spanish cooking
Hang-gliding
Parrot fever
Botulism
Russian roulette
Parachuting
Suicide in someone else's house
IRA own goal
Eaten by a pike
Racing a Right Nigel from Oxford to Cambridge in a
silly sports car
Heroin overdose
Alcohol overdose
Shooting accident swinging down the line (see *Naff
Things To Do When Staying In The Country*)
Executed as a mercenary
Bored to death by wife
Cardiac arrest during rigorous keep-fit programme
Bee stings
Sun burn

NAFF MEDICAL APPLIANCES

Trusses
Incontinence pants
Corn plasters
Surgical stockings
Colostomy bags

NAFF MEDICAL APPLIANCES

Stomach-pumps (see Godfrey Smith)
Reinforced leopard-skin bikini (see Jean Rook)
Dr Scholl shoes (at least he's making a lot of money out
of the Germans)

—6—
GETTING AWAY FROM IT ALL

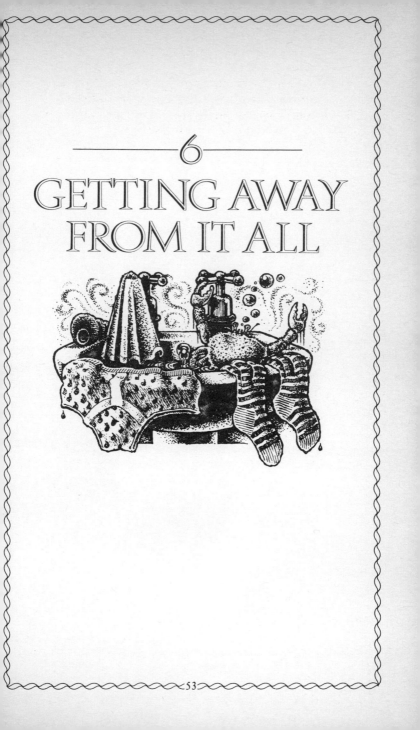

NAFF HOLIDAYS

Benidorm

Blackpool

Majorca

Jersey

St Tropez

Costa Brava

Tunisia

Corfu

Mykonos

Morocco

Miami

The Canary Isles

Exchanging houses with family in Brussels

Climbing Snowdon

Camping in Normandy

Pony trekking

Going from London to Oxford in humorously painted barge

Caravanning, unless registered gipsy

Pot-holing

Golfing in the Algarve

Slaughtering wildlife in the Highlands (see Max Hastings and *Naff Things The Royal Family Do*).

Townsend Thoreson cruises, esp. to Sweden

Eight secretaries sharing a villa in Portugal

Staying with Emma Soames in Cairo

Walking along Offa's Dyke

Cruising on the Norfolk Broads

Taking the family to Portrush, Ulster. Richard West writes: 'Portrush is agreeably old-fashioned compared to most English seaside resorts. There are no blacks, punks, skinheads, mods or oiks. There are very few foreigners except for the well-mannered Chinese restaurateurs. No obvious gays, but much obvious gaiety. No porn shops but lots of traditional "what-the-butler-saw" machines and saucy postcards.'

(See *Naff Hacks* and *Naff Saloon-bar Philosophers*)

Treading in the footsteps of Boswell and the immortal Sam in Scotland (see *Naff Metropolitan Critics*)

NAFF AIRLINES

Aeroflot
Air Pakistan
Air Lingus
Pan Am (hostesses with bad legs)
Air Vietnam
Korean Airways
British Caledonian (paradoxically, they have the
best commercials)
All Third World airlines

NAFF THINGS TO DO ON AN AEROPLANE

Hijack it
Read *Screen International*
Read a Jeffrey Archer novel
Send an erotic note to the pilot
Have an anxiety attack
Fail to tranquilise a screaming baby
Talk to neighbour
Travel under a false name (see *Naff Couples*)
Join the Mile High Club (see *Naff Clubs*)
Read *Fear of Flying* (suggests you want to join the Mile
High Club)
Wear a personalised sleeping mask
Read *High Life*
Allow yourself to be intimidated by the cabin staff
Bully the cabin staff
Get drunk on free alcohol
Travel in large, boisterous, all-female holiday party
Snore

NAFF THINGS THE ENGLISH
DO ON A BEACH

Read the *Daily Telegraph*
Play cricket
Wear knotted handkerchiefs
Paddle
Complain about the heat
Build sandcastles
Bury parents
Drink out of beer-cans
Shrimp
Undress clumsily under towel
Talk about computers
Overdo it on first day
Read novels by Jeffrey Archer
Discuss Test Match score
Surreptitiously photograph topless Swedish secretaries
oiling one another's tanned, ballooning buttocks
Have heart-attacks as a result of surreptious
photography

NAFF THINGS GERMANS
DO ON A BEACH

Throw frisbees
Form human pyramids
Throw things into the sea for half-witted dogs to
retrieve
Barge to the front of beach-bar queues
Talk in German
Run very fast into the sea from great distances,
splashing English paddlers
Drip on you
Bounce volley-balls against you
Drink beer all day and then waddle only crutch-high
into the sea to urinate like horses. At least the English
pretend to swim about a bit

NAFF THINGS THE FRENCH DO ON A BEACH

Undress without attempting discretion
Display enormous pubic bushes
Urinate against rocks
Encourage precocious, bikinied tots to behave cutely

NAFF WAYS OF GOING ROUND THE WORLD

On a Cunard cruise
In a facetiously decorated London taxi
On a bicycle
Walking for charity
In a balloon
Roller-skating for Jesus

NAFF COUNTRIES

Belgium
Canada

NAFF WEATHER CONDITIONS

Unsettled outlook (esp. with sunny intervals)
Occasional rain
Poor visibility
Fresh easterly winds

NAFF WEATHER ZONES

Foulness
Dogger

NAFF DAYS

Sunday
Boxing Day
August Bank Holiday
Mother's Day
Vera Day

NAFF TIMES OF THE DAY

10.50 a.m.
2.45 p.m.

NAFF THINGS TO DO WHEN STAYING IN THE COUNTRY

Be at stool within two hours of arrival
Introduce yourself to the butler
Wash socks in the basin
Not return to London till Monday morning
Shoot fox
Arrive with vinyl luggage and nightclub hostess
Demur at butchery
Phone New Zealand
Wear a new fisherman's hat
Refuse to play games after dinner
Shiver
Get up at lunchtime
Shoot down the line (see *Naff Causes of Death*)
Claim another man's partridge
Refer to hounds as dogs
Throw-up on being blooded
Refer to hunting pink as red coat (Redcoats work at
Butlins)
Offer to help with the washing-up
Arrive with bottle of wine for hostess
Offer to pay for phone calls

NAFF THINGS TO DO WHEN STAYING IN THE COUNTRY

Carve up lawn with mini-Hondas
Fall into the moat
Display cowardice when asked to round up cattle
Be unable to tell a hawk from a handsaw (esp. when
wind is westerly)
Mistake laird for gillie
Display ignorance about hedges
Talk too little

—7—
HIGH FINANCE

NAFF CREDIT CARDS

Access

NAFF INVESTMENTS

Unit Trusts
Granny Bonds
Property
Local authority bonds
Premium bonds
Stamps
Pension schemes
The computer revolution
Lease on passport–photo machine

NAFF WAYS OF MAKING MONEY

Marrying it
Buying debts
Begging
Busking
Bondwashing
Selling clothes pegs
Selling your memoirs to the *People*
Snouting for the police
Snouting for a gossip columnist (esp. Nigel Dempster)
Writing dirty jokes for 'That's Life'
Collecting on used bottles

NAFF WAYS OF GOING BANKRUPT

Running a business efficiency school
Running a brothel
Busking

NAFF WAYS OF GOING BANKRUPT

Running an English pub in Majorca (esp. if called 'Los Dos Caballeros Ingleses')

With the concession on a defective space-invaders machine

Running a protection racket

Confounded by a rise in the mortgage rate

NAFF AMOUNTS OF MONEY TO GO BANKRUPT FOR

£3,011 to Access

£18,964 to the Inland Revenue

£57,829 to members of Equity

£203,167,961 to stranded holiday-makers

NAFF SMALL MEN

The small investor

The small businessman

The small saver

The small-holder

The small, but vocal, minority

Willie Carson

Jack Tinker

Sir Michael Edwardes

Paul Anka

8
BETWEEN THE SHEETS

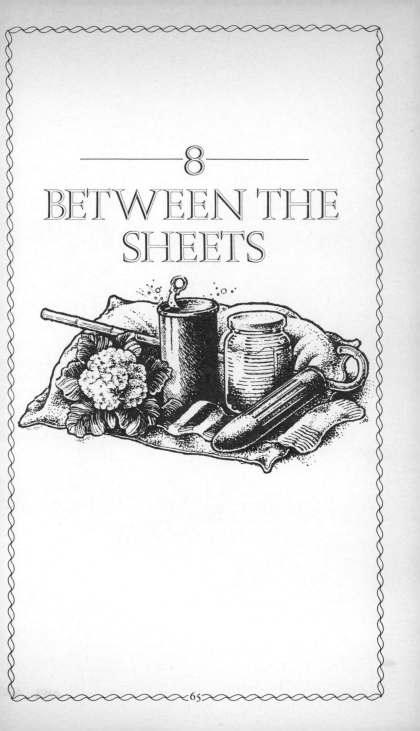

NAFF AGES TO LOSE VIRGINITY

HIM

12

26

HER

8

13

50

NAFF PLACES TO LOSE VIRGINITY

The back of a car

The front of a car

Behind the Rialto

Behind the Bar Magnifico, Benidorm, with an excitable
Spanish waiter

Standing up in the Seven Sisters Road

On a dance floor

In parents' bed

In a rugger scrum

On Wimbledon Common (see *Naff Things To Do On
Wimbledon Common*)

NAFF SEXUAL PRACTICES

Paying for it

Not paying for it if you've agreed to

Dial-an-enema

Dressing in wife's pantyhose when she's out shopping

Le vice anglais

Not faking orgasm (nobody gets to sleep)

Faking orgasm too obviously

Post-mortems. Tears. Confessions. The blues
(post-coital)

The blues (pre-coital)

Talking about it on TV (see Anna Raeburn and Clive
James and *Naff Para-sexual Activities*)

NAFF SEXUAL PRACTICES

Wearing a scrotum-grip to increase penis size
Sticking things up members of the Monday Club (see
Naff Clubs and *Naff Call-girls*)
Wearing humorous condoms, esp. with Union Jack
motif
Inflating scrotum to the size of a tennis ball
Using cunnilingual aids, esp. strawberry or peppermint
flavour

NAFF PLACES TO HAVE SEX

In lifts
On the snooker table at Stocks
In the jacuzzi at Stocks
In an aeroplane lavatory with air-hostess (see *Naff Clubs*)
In the Dorchester, under false name, with temporary
secretary
In Los Angeles

NAFF PRE-SEXUAL ACTIVITY

HIM
Taking socks off last
Getting on top straight away
Boasting
Chatting
Confessing prior matrimony
Leaving underwear or socks on
Failing to remove family photographs
Failing to remove depraved photographs
Getting drunk
Getting her drunk

HER
Applying face-cream
Laughing

Inspecting cellulite
Discussing obstetrics
Displaying operation scar
Shivering
Getting under sheets
Turning lights off

NAFF FOREPLAY

Grappling on sofa
Pinching
Tickling
Baby-talk
Saying: 'How do you like it?'
Assuming strange accents
Growling like a dog (if female)

NAFF SEXUAL ACTIVITY

Writhing automatically
Gouging
Raking
Talking
Sneezing
Giggling
Expressing disappointment with progress
Removing teeth prior to cunnilingus, or, worse, fellatio
Penetrating too quickly
Losing it
Biting too hard
Squashing
Deciding against it
His being penetrated, esp. if Member of the Monday
Club (see *Naff Clubs*)
Premature ejaculation (see *Naff Ways Of Avoiding
Premature Ejaculation*)

NAFF WAYS OF AVOIDING PREMATURE EJACULATION

Masturbating in the afternoon
Thinking about your VAT returns
Thinking about Shirley Conran

NAFF PRE-CLIMACTIC BEHAVIOUR

Groaning noisily
Informing partner of progress
She asking him if he's seen to the insurance yet

NAFF THINGS TO DO AT POINT OF ORGASM

Burst into tears (esp. him)
Break wind
Fall out
Be sick
Cry out wrong name (esp. wrong sex) or 'Mother!'
Answer phone

NAFF THINGS TO THINK ABOUT AT POINT OF ORGASM

Newsreaders, esp. Sandy Gall
Nurses
Policewomen
SS officers
Pop stars
School mistresses
Schoolgirls
Elderly actresses
The Royal Family
Sylvester Stallone
Erika Roe

NAFF STREAKERS

All female streakers are naff. No male streakers are naff,
least of all stupendously well-hung men who invade the
pitch at a Test Match and upset Richie Benaud

NAFF POST-SEXUAL ACTIVITY

Not paying for it if you've agreed to
Confessing
Weeping
Watching replay on video
Showing video to friends
Blackmailing partner
Writing about the episode in the Sunday papers (see *Naff
Groupies*)

NAFF PARA-SEXUAL ACTIVITY

HER

Writing about it in *Cosmopolitan* (see *Naff Magazines*)
Riding
Eating
Watching wrestling on TV
Displaying legs on 'The Morecambe And Wise Show'
Talking about it on the radio (see Anna Raeburn)
Reading the *News Of The World*
Reading *Lace*
Telling dirty jokes on TV (see Esther Rantzen)
Dancing on own in self-adoring way in a discotheque
Walking around in the nude
Telling humorous anecdotes about her tits on 'The
Parkinson Show' (see Diana Rigg)
Having a massage in the early afternoon from a tattooed
Turk

NAFF PARA-SEXUAL ACTIVITY

HIM

Working for the *News Of The World*
Telling jokes
Walking in Wales
Writing dirty letters to *Forum*
Climbing mountains
Singing Rugby songs
Playing squash
Pillow-fighting
Arm-wrestling
Surreptitious photography in Hyde Park, esp. of
schoolgirls
Being a schoolmaster
Walking around semi-erect
Verbally groping starlets on chatshows (see
Michael Parkinson)

NAFF SEXUAL MYTHS

Excessive interest in women suggests homosexual
tendencies
Excessive promiscuity suggests loneliness and probable
impotency fears
Penis size is unimportant
Blacks are no better at it than any other racial group
Promiscuous women are searching angrily for love (see
Naff Things Agony Aunts Say)
Women sometimes like to be taken roughly from
behind in the kitchen
Pepsi-Cola is a spermicide

NAFF SEXUAL AFFLICTIONS

Premature ejaculation
Hung like a haggis
Hung like a cocktail sausage

NAFF SEXUAL STIMULANTS

Spanish fly
Talking dirty
Driving fast
Pretending to be a virgin
Pretending to be homosexual

NAFF VISUAL AIDS

Health and Efficiency
Fiesta
Sadie Stern
Butcher Shop magazines
Deep Throat
The Story of O
All blue films, esp. Swedish or American
Country Life Book of Diana, Princess of Wales, by Lornie
Leete-Jones, Country Life Books, £8.95

NAFF SEXUAL EUPHEMISMS

'Make love to me!'
Down there
Winkle
Your thing
My thing
Obstetrical ailment
Social disease
Hanky-panky
Leg-over situation

NAFF PLACES TO MASTURBATE

In a sauna
In a sock

NAFF PLACES TO MASTURBATE

In a confessional
On a tiled bathroom floor
In a vegetable
Beside your sleeping wife
In the cinema
Wimbledon No. 1 Court during the final of The
Ladies' Plate

NAFF LUBRICANTS

Vaseline
Vick
Spittle
KY jelly
Butter

NAFF NUMBER OF TIMES TO DO IT PER CALENDAR MONTH

250
1

NAFF THINGS TO DO IN A SAUNA

Wear socks
Talk
Become tumescent
Come out

NAFF PLACES TO COME OUT

On 'The Parkinson Show' (see Graham Chapman)
In conversation with one's parents

In a pulpit
In No. 1 Court at the Old Bailey

NAFF HETEROSEXUALS

Sir Nicholas Fairbairn (see *Naff Politicians*)
Michael Parkinson
Alan Whicker
Clive James
Geoffrey Dickens (see *Naff Politicians*)
Sir William Piggot-Brown
Bruce Forsyth
Reginald Bosanquet
Taki
Jeffrey Bernard
Lord Lambton

NAFF EX-WOMANISERS

Errol Flynn
Frank Harris
Pope Alexander VI
Malcolm Muggeridge
Talullah Bankhead

NAFF HILARIOUS GIVE-AWAYS

'Why is it that when people become interested in writing
or reading about physical sex they seem to be caught up
in an obsession? And why does the obsession seem to
centre on every conceivable departure from the loving
act of sex in marriage? Sex before marriage, sex out of
marriage, oral sex . . .'
Christopher Booker. (Bad luck, Mrs Booker. See *Naff
Philosophers*)

9
THE OLDEST PROFESSION

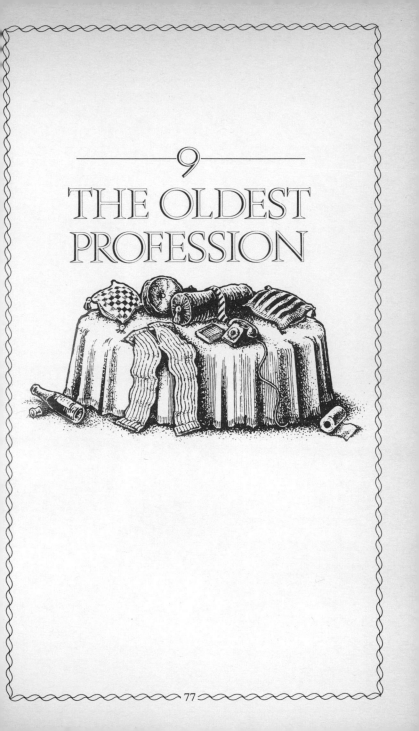

NAFF THINGS PUNTERS DO

Offer foreplay
Kiss
Talk
Ask her out to dinner

NAFF THINGS PUNTERS SAY

'What made you take up this way of life?'
'I'd like to get to know you as a person.'
'Does your husband/boyfriend know you do this?'
'I love you.'

NAFF MADAMES

All madames are naff except Madame Claude, and even she's a little naff

NAFF CALL-GIRLS

All who work the Stork Club, but paradoxically not Chaplin's
All who advertise in tobacconists' windows, phone boxes or *Where To Go In London*
All who work the lobby of the Cumberland Hotel, but not the Hilton
Norma Levy
Xaviera Hollander
Fat Antoinette
Moscow Road Pat
All who live in Nell Gwynn House and Chelsea Cloisters, but paradoxically not Dolphin Square, which is very handy for the House of Commons

NAFF THINGS PEOPLE SAY ABOUT PROSTITUTES

A necessary evil

If it wasn't for them decent women wouldn't be able to walk the streets

'She has been a prostitute from such an early age that she now thinks it is perfectly normal to have sex with men.'
Superintendent Mellor of the West Midlands Police

'I once came across a prostitute in Singapore. I chatted to her for a while and soon discovered that she was a human being like the rest of us. Her eyes told me this.'
Graham Greene

NAFF THINGS NIGHTCLUB HOSTESSES DO

Cheat you
Rob you
Kick you
Order champagne
Give you crabs

10

THE MATRIMONIAL SCENE

NAFF STAG PARTY BEHAVIOUR

Boot–blacking genitals (esp. the bride's)

Debagging the groom, each other, waiters, nightclub doormen, taxi-drivers, policemen, old actors on way home after the show

Behaving so badly that old Bill is forced to give you a kicking in a shop doorway

Lighting farts

Handcuffing naked groom to railings

Reciting limericks

Beating yourself up

Beating the bride up

NAFF PLACES TO SPEND YOUR WEDDING NIGHT

With bride's mother

With friends

In the bridal suite at the Cunard Hotel (see *Naff Hotels*)

Dover

Charing Cross Hospital, esp. in maternity ward

West End Central Police Station

Under a table at the Stork Club

NAFF NAMES FOR THE WIFE

The wife

The better half

Mother

La Dolce Vita

Her ladyship

Madam

Mrs Mouse

Smelly poos

Her indoors

NAFF NAMES FOR THE HUSBAND

Himself
The old man
The head of the house
The breadwinner of the family
Big boy

NAFF THINGS COUPLES DO
TO PASS THE TIME

Competitive dancing (esp. ice-dancing)
Go for a drive on Sunday
Go to the pub
Eat out once a week in an Indian restaurant
Learn Spanish
Play scrabble
Talk to the cats instead of each other
Collaborate on a TV series (see Terence Brady and
Charlotte Bingham)
Go shopping together on Saturday
Spend Sunday in bed together
Travel
Share the parenting

11
MEANINGFUL RELATIONSHIPS

NAFF FIRST DATE DIFFICULTIES

What to wear?
Wet palms
Spontaneous emissions
Impotence
Being stood up
Getting the wrong sister
Not knowing when (or whether) to make a move
Passing out
Not knowing whether the opposition really cares about you as a human being
Succumbing through not knowing how to refuse (esp. disagreeable for men)
Crashing the car

NAFF THINGS WOMEN SAY

'Flats don't clean themselves, you know'
'Have you seen to the insurance yet?'
'If I've told you once I've told you a thousand times'
'I hope you don't think you're going to sleep'
'*Mothers* can't go on strike, you know'
'The bath mat's wet again'
'Do come in, the kettle's on'
'He tried to get into my pants'
'Why's that man looking at me?'
'I'm leaving you! You're contemptible! You're not even a man!'
'Wait and seeeee!'
'I don't care what he does as long as I don't know about it'
'You don't love me any more'
'I haven't got anything to wear'
'You never take me out any more'
(To daughter with sickening wink) 'You can ask the old man for anything this morning!'

NAFF THINGS MEN SAY

'I bet you'd be good between the sheets!'

'I'd love to talk to you about your career but right now I'd like to fuck your brains out'

'Would you girls like me to turn on the jacuzzi for you?'

'Wrong time of the month, darling?'

'Drink up!'

'Are there any more at home like you?'

'Have you ever thought of being a model?'

'What you need is a damned good screw'

'If you didn't want to be picked up why are you wearing so much make-up/a low-cut dress/a skirt that shows your knickers?'

'Of *course* I'll look after you'

'I'm not being unreasonable, am I?'

'When a lady says "no", she means "perhaps"; when she says "perhaps", she means "yes"; when she says "yes", she's no lady.' Lord Denning (see *Naff Judges*)

NAFF THINGS WOMEN DO

Shop

Wear red rubber gloves to do the washing-up

Cook

Nag

Lick handkerchiefs and scrub faces

Potter

Purse lips

Do the housework

Weep obscurely in the middle of the night

Clench their faces

Fail derisorily to respond to sexual advances

Fail to produce orgasm

Blame man for failure to produce orgasm

Demand sex from exhausted, headache-ridden husband

Have sterile best friend's baby for her

Compete embarrassingly with each other for men
Sneer at women younger than themselves
Go around in pretty/plain couples
Dance round their handbags
Get fat
Stand by their husbands

NAFF THINGS MEN DO

Drink milk straight from the bottle
Stand on the bathmat
Tell jokes
Fail to clean baths, basins, etc. after use
Make fatuous boasts
Never say anything
Demand fellatio
Glare
Pout
Groan
Sulk
Burst into tears
Scratch scrotum
Check flies
Get drunk and tell wife's best friend he loves her
Evade the truth
Forget the truth
Fantasize about what they could have done if only . . .
Play soccer
Play low-grade rugger
Wash car
Mow lawn
Kick the cat
Improve the house (esp. the guttering, whatever that is)
Flatulate stupefyingly
Quote chunks from 'Casablanca'

Naff Things Women Know

When you won't feel the benefit
When you've had enough
When your dental appointment's due
If you read in a bad light you'll strain your eyes
That boys make you sicker than girls in pregnancy
How long things keep in a freezer
How to remove stains
That all the goodness in a potato is in the skin
101 things to do with an egg
Paradoxically, not when you've been unfaithful to them
with their best friend

Naff Things Men Know

Where to get a drink after closing
How to catch the barman's eye
How to get the little lady in the mood
How to carve
How to start a car with a flat battery
The short-cut to Gatwick avoiding the snarl-up on the
A324 by going through Mitcham
The nearest VD clinic
How to tell a funny story
The team Ron Greenwood should have picked
The Goon scripts by heart
That there's nothing to be ashamed of in making a profit
That the police are doing a good job under impossible
circumstances
That all feminists are lesbians
That politics and sport don't mix (see *Naff Philosophical
Theories*)
That six of the best never did anyone any harm (see *Naff
Sexual Practices*)
That Denis Thatcher is really a very intelligent man in
his own right. How else could he have made so much
money?

NAFF DEAR JOHNS

'I've been thinking about us . . .'
'We're not going anywhere . . .'
'You'll always be very special to me'
'I hope we can always be friends'
'I'm leaving you, Simon. I want to discover who I really am'

NAFF AMERICAN KISS-OFF LINES

'It's a wrap, babe'
'We're not in the same head-space'
'I don't understand where you're coming from'

NAFF KISS-OFF PRESENTS

A leading role in 'Crossroads' (see *Naff Couples*)
An introduction to Jack Nicholson
1st class tickets to Hawaii for you and your mother
A Porsche 924
A BMW 520
A diamond bracelet (paradoxically, not a diamond necklace, which is a sign of enthusiasm)

—12—
IN SOCIETY

NAFF PARTIES

Bottle

Wine and cheese (esp. Tenants' Association Meet Your
Neighbour)

Coffee mornings, esp. in NW1 and South Chingford

Fondue

Pyjama (see *Naff Para-Sexual Activities*)

Any party attended by both Paula Yates *and* Janet
Street-Porter

The *Mail On Sunday* launch

Any party involving the flying of guests to a foreign
country (esp. Switzerland) at host's expense (see Jocelyn
Stevens and *Naff Couples*)

All office parties, esp. the *Cosmopolitan* Christmas party
(see *Naff Magazines* and *Naff Editorials*)

Arianna Stassinopoulous's fiftieth birthday party for
Bernard Levin

All fancy dress parties (see *Naff Things To Go To A
Fancy Dress Party As*)

All theme parties, esp. 'tarts and vicars'

All publishing parties, esp. if held in the Chamber of
Horrors at Madame Tussauds

Wedding receptions held in the Park Lane Hotel,
Piccadilly

All Victor Lownes's parties

All parties held on a boat on the Thames

All hen parties with a male stripper as cabaret

All birthday parties held in a restaurant

All stag parties

All regimental or school reunions

The Conservative Party

Any 21st birthday dance given in a marquee for a man in
the Green Belt with catering by Searcy's

All promotional parties, esp. held for no discoverable
reason at Brands Hatch

Street parties (esp. Jubilee Year)

All party-bookings for rotten musicals, esp. 'Annie' (see
Naff Musicals)

All wife-swapping parties, esp. those involving the
'knickers in the washing-machine game', unless the
altered arrangements become permanent

NAFF THINGS TO GO TO A FANCY DRESS PARTY AS

Antony and Cleopatra
Alice and the Mad Hatter
Julius Caesar
Hitler
A potato

NAFF DANCES

Clog
Belly
Morris
Pasa Doble
Flamenco
Tea Dances
Ladies Excuse me (see Martina Navratilova)
The Hokey Cokey (but not the Lambeth Walk)
The Gay Gordons (see *Naff Regiments*)
The dance of the silly cygnets in Swan Lake
The conga (esp. if performed by Germans)
The last waltz

NAFF CLUBS

The RAC (admits women and children)
The Oxford and Cambridge
The Mile High (see *Naff Things To Do On An Aeroplane*)
The Savile
The Pitt, Cambridge
Heaven
The Embassy
The Gateways
The White Elephant
Lenny's Video Club, off the Old Kent Road
The Bristol Suite

The Monday Club (see *Naff Sexual Activity*)
Wentworth Golf Club (racist)
Bodys
The Victoria Sporting Club
The Liberal Club
The Ranelagh Yacht Club
The Clermont
The Cavalry
Studio 54
Plato's Retreat
The Arts Theatre Club
The Dangerous Sports

NAFF ASSOCIATIONS

The Association of Circus Proprietors of Great Britain
The National Viewers and Listeners Association
The Society of West End Theatres
The Women's Gas Federation and Young Homemakers
The Guild of Professional After Dinner Speakers
The Freedom Association
The Aims of Industry
The Pipe-Jacking Association
The British Man-Made Fibres Federation
The National Council Of Women Of Great Britain
ASH
PUSSI
The Responsible Society
The Lord's Day Observance Society
The Freedom in Sport Society (see *Naff Philosophical Theories*)

13
THE ART OF CONVERSATION

NAFF CONVERSATIONAL TOPICS

IN A PUB

Politics – sod 'em
Women – bless 'em
Drink – what's yours?
Money
Cars
Football
Racing
Your rights
Imperial themes in Renaissance and baroque art

AT A DINNER PARTY

The last episode of 'Minder', esp. if you saw it
Marital sex
Mortgages
Holidays
Children
Education
Diarrhoea
Brown sugar
The F–Plan diet
Mechanically recovered meat
DIY
Hi–fi
Living in Clerkenwell
Mysticism
The unions
Herpes
Double glazing
What time it would be rude to leave

IN A LAUNDERETTE

The price of things
Anxiety attacks
Operations
Conspiracy theories
Sensitivity

IN A LAUNDERETTE

Fassbinder
Privilege
The police state we live in
God was a spaceman

ON A BUS

Race relations
Hanging's too good for them

WITH YOUR BUTCHER

Wine
Fish
Princess Di

WITH YOUR PSYCHIATRIST

Underfelt
Your eating holiday in the Dordogne
His bill

WITH YOUR MOTHER

Your homosexuality
Her sex life
Oral sex

AT A PARTY

Jokes (telling them)
Feminism
Television
Jerry and Mick
What star sign are you?
Where do you live?
My job
Your job
Your tan
My car
Your body
My brain
Your place
Or mine?

WITH CAB DRIVERS
Good old Enoch
The IRA

NAFF TO MENTION

Margaret Thatcher to Ted Heath
Ronnie Biggs to Slipper of the Yard
Auberon Waugh to Gore Vidal
Lady Tryon to Princess Di
Face-lifts to 'Bubbles' Rothermere
Hitler's Diaries to Lord Dacre
Police corruption to Anna Raeburn
Lady Antonia Fraser to Clive James
What foreign correspondents do for laughs when
abroad to Mary Kenny
Adam Faith to John Lloyd
The younger generation to Mrs Whitehouse
Christopher Booker to Patrick Marnham
Water sports to Richard Ingrams

NAFF CATCH-PHRASES

'Nick, nick!'
'It's the way I tell 'em!'
'You're on your own, Balliol'
'My husband and I . . .'
'Book him, Danno. Murder one'

NAFF THINGS TO MAKE JOKES ABOUT

British Leyland
Spanish plumbing
Motorway food

NAFF THINGS TO MAKE JOKES ABOUT

British Rail sandwiches
Des O'Connor's singing
Michael Foot's clothes
Tony Benn
Ken Livingstone
'King' Arthur Scargill
Mary Whitehouse
Traffic wardens
Polish goalkeepers
Third-world television (see Clive James)
'Crossroads'
The Sex Olympics
The Egyptian army
Italy's performance in the last war
Harry Carpenter
Nicholas Parsons
Harold Wilson's vanity
Zsa Zsa Gabor's husbands
Dean Martin's drinking
Hampstead intellectuals
Silly place-names (viz Wagglewater – see Arthur
Marshall)
Roy Jenkins's claret drinking
Personal defects, deformities and misfortunes
Cyril Smith's figure
Sir Keith Joseph's eyes
Ted Heath's laugh
Margaret Thatcher's voice
Godfrey Smith's column
Richard Ingrams's television reviews
Jean Rook's tits

NAFF BOASTS

'But then, of course, I left university without a degree. I
like to think I have a First from the School of Hard
Knocks'

'But then I'm one of those people who always buy their underwear at Marks and Sparks'

'But then I'm an incurable romantic'

'But then I don't pretend to understand economics'

'But then I was hopeless at mathematics at school'

'Happily, I'm the sort of person who can laugh at himself' (see Jeffrey Bernard)

'Being bullied by petty bureaucrats has never been my strong point, I'm afraid'

'I'm afraid I'm one of those people who are too honest for their own good'

'*I* still think in shillings'

'Of course, you're talking to someone who slept through Olivier's Hamlet'

'I took a degree in trigonometry but I still can't tell uphill from down'

'I'm absolutely *hopeless* with money'

'I haven't been inside a church since I was confirmed'

'I don't believe in organised religion or anything like that, but I count myself a Christian'

'I'm afraid I've got one of those maddeningly logical minds'

'I saw 'Deep Throat'. Frankly I fell asleep'

'I was utterly *hopeless* at games at school. Luckily I was saved from being bullied by my sense of humour'

'Of course I've tried coke, but quite frankly it did nothing for me at all'

'If Jack Nicholson asked *me* for a date, I'd tell him to get lost'

'The *New Statesman*? Good heavens. I haven't looked at it since Arthur Marshall left. He had me in fits of laughter'

'But then you're talking to someone who never got past page three of *Das Kapital*' (Especially naff if said by Labour politician)

'My book wasn't meant to be a deep sociological tract. I wrote it as simple family entertainment, a romp, if you

like. If the critics didn't care for it, that's just too bad. I
didn't write it for them'

'Where could I go after Mick? Robert could buy him out
ten times over'

'Required reading at Kensington Palace, home of Princess Margaret, the Prince and Princess of Wales and
Prince and Princess Michael of Kent, the Mail Diary
received an unsolicited testimonial yesterday from within. "When we read your column here, we all look at each
other and wonder which of us has been talking to you," I
was told. "It's as if you had been present in the room –
your stories are quite uncanny".'

Nigel Dempster

NAFF RUMOURS

The CIA and the Mafia conspired to kill President
Kennedy

The Kennedys contracted to have Marilyn Monroe
killed

The head of MI5 is always a Soviet mole

Pepsi-Cola financed the invasion of Afghanistan

Lloyds Bank runs the world-wide heroin trade

The Foreign Office conspired with Argentina over the
invasion of the Falklands

Ration cards are being printed in Britain

There are giant albino crocodiles in the New York
sewers

Alexander Haig was Deep Throat

Edward VIII was a Nazi collaborator

The Duke of Clarence was Jack the Ripper

The brain behind the Great Train Robbery was never
caught

All French film actresses worked at one time for
Madame Claude (see *Naff Madames*)

Six men and forty-five horses were killed during the
filming of the chariot race in 'Ben Hur'

You can make pot out of banana skins

There are more gangsters buried under the Hammersmith flyover than you'll ever see having a jar in The Water Rat on a Saturday night

A black mamba can bring down a horse galloping at 30 m.p.h.

There is a secret service so secret that even the Home Secretary doesn't know about it.

Mrs Thatcher has concentration camps ready for the workers

The Tories are deliberately prolonging the troubles in Ulster to train the army

NAFF INSIDE KNOWLEDGE

All-in wrestling's fixed

The charts are fixed

Decca turned down the Beatles

Everyone turned down *The Day Of The Jackal*

Diana Dors' real name is Clunt

Keith Richards has had his blood changed five times

Where he put the Mars Bar

The SAS fought in Vietnam

Lord Snowdon is hung like a horse

Clint Eastwood is hung like a hamster

Cliff Richard isn't gay

Morecambe and Wise can't stand each other

The true identity of the notorious judge, whom *Private Eye* grassed up as being a client of Lindi St Clair, the celebrated call-girl

Bob Monkhouse is a highly intelligent man

If you inform Chelsea police that you're going away on holiday your house will be burglarised

Paul Newman's only 4ft 9ins

Charles Bronson is 69 this year

Miles Copeland still works for the CIA

Rupert Murdoch is a Roman Catholic

Jean Rook really *has* got a degree in English Literature

Nigel Dempster really *does* think he's doing an important job

Paul Halloran keeps his job on *Private Eye* because he's 'got something' on Richard Ingrams

Tina Brown knows what it is but she's not saying

The reason why Tina Brown isn't saying

NAFF LINES OF POETRY TO KNOW IF YOU DON'T KNOW ANY MORE

'Cap'n art thou sleeping there below?'

'You're a better man than I am, Gunga Din'

'Had we but world enough and time'

'Hail to thee blithe spirit, Bird thou never wert . . .'

'I must go down to the sea again'

'I wandered lonely as a cloud'

'Once more into the breach dear friends . . .'

'Stout Cortez . . .'

'Come friendly bombs and drop on Slough . . .'

'They fuck you up your mum and dad . . .'

NAFF THINGS PEOPLE CALL FEMINISTS

Strident

Lesbian

Impressively moustachioed

NAFF THINGS FEMINISTS SAY

Male reasonableness is a form of rape
Pornography prostitutes all women
Men invented language and use it to oppress women
Marriage is merely legalised rape

NAFF WAYS TO ADDRESS
A BLACK BUS CONDUCTOR

Captain
Squire
Chief

14
OUT AND ABOUT

NAFF RESTAURANTS

Mimmo d'Ischia, 61 Elizabeth Street, SW1. Poor man's Meridiana

Meridiana, 169 Fulham Road, SW3. Poor man's San Frediano

San Frediano, 62 Fulham Road, SW3. Poor man's San Lorenzo

San Lorenzo, 22 Beauchamp Place, SW3. Sun Page Three girls and jeans manufacturers

La Famiglia, 7 Langton Street, SW10. Puffettes quacking at free-loading journalists

Eleven Park Walk, SW10. Hairdressers, underwear designers and *Ritz* readers (paradoxically, the food isn't too bad)

The Terrazza, 19 Romilly Street, W1. Sixties film producers and advertising agents lying to one another

Cranks, 8 Marshall Street. Loonies and left-wing food

Tiberio's, 22 Queen Street, W1. Actually has a band! (Or it did the last time anyone went there)

The Gasworks, Waterford Road, SW6. Thieves, tarts, Old Etonians and, paradoxically, delicious food

Lockets, Marsham Street, SW1. Facetious menu and Roy Hattersley stuffing himself in a corner

The Hard Rock Cafe, 150 Old Park Lane, W1. Wilfully out of date

The Golden Stool of Ashanti, 133 Wells Street, E9. An executive-style restaurant with African decor

The Ivy, 1 West Street, WC2. Since Lord Grade bought it for the wife, you could fire off a cannon and not hit one old theatrical tart. Full now of fat marketing men with digital watches

The Suntory, 72 St James Street, SW1. Surly Nippons and pulverising bills

M'sieur Frog, 31a Essex Road, N1. Bustling with Gallic charm. Proprietors: Howard and Tina Rawlinson and Philip Snuggs.

The Lotus House, Edgware Road. Rag-trade night out

NAFF THINGS TO DO IN A RESTAURANT

Go dutch

Go drunk to table having spent too much time at bar

Order wine on sitting down

Address wine waiter as 'captain'

Say 'chop chop!' to Chinese waiter

Hang coat on back of chair

Smoke a pipe

Table-hop (see Camilla Horne)

Ask for celebrities' autographs

Send message via waiter to blonde in corner

Arrive with dogs, children etc.

Ask for separate checks

Knock off service charge

Squabble over disparities in joint bill

Ask management to turn the music up

Spend much time on telephone (incoming calls)

Strip off under the table (see Pamela Stephenson)

Be forced to surrender your table at eight-thirty

Have birthday cake brought to table

Order strawberries out of season and then complain
about the price

Talk too loudly about your money, your sex life, your
friends, your bowels

Call French waiter 'garçon'

Offer owner protection

On being told to 'piss off, son', threaten owner with
solicitor's letter

Snap fingers at waiters to attract attention

Start a fight (see Peter Langan)

Insist on buying one cigarette (see Basil Seal)

Breast-feed your baby (see Esther Rantzen)

Drink spirits with food

Fold napkin

Use pengrip on knife

Cut Stilton down

Continually thank the waiter

Dunk moustache in soup and suck it

Take a line in the Ladies

NAFF RESTAURANT CRITICS

All restaurant critics are naff except Basil Seal

NAFF FOOD

Prawn cocktail
Melon and Parma ham
Avocado and prawns
Florida cocktail
Grapefruit cocktail
Escalope Milanaise
Chicken-in-the-basket
Scampi
Doner kebabs
Coupe Jacques
Chicken fried rice
All curries
Paella-in-the-packet
Beef-boil-in-a-bag
Duck à l'orange
Chili con carne
Fish fingers
Gammon steak
Egg mayonnaise
Whelks
Duchess potatoes
Wiener Schnitzel
Pickled onions
Dips
Crisps
Cornish pasties
Mixed grill
Walls pork pies
Parsnip pie
Trifle
Compressed turkey in a tin
Eggs Florentine

NAFF FOOD

Tomato soup (unless real)
Popcorn
Individual fruit pies

NAFF BREADS

Spanish
Russian
Mother's Pride

NAFF HOTELS

The Mayfair
The Piccadilly
The Penta
The Churchill
The Cunard International
The Cumberland
The Regent Palace
The Strand Palace
The Hilton
The Tara
The Ritz

NAFF BEHAVIOUR IN HOTELS

Not pay the bill
Set fire to the furniture (see *Naff Dead Pop Stars*)
Sneak thieve
Solicit in the lobby
Supply own product – Allbran, decaffeinated coffee,
etc. – at breakfast
Offer to pay bill in advance

Wash own clothes and hang them out of the window

Wash elaborately stained sheets in the bath

Fall down the laundry chute

Make own bed

Steal towels and coathangers

Tip the manager (paradoxically, it's not naff to tip Lord
Matthews at the Ritz – a mistake anyone could make)

Ask the night manager for girls

Ask the chambermaid if she'd ever thought of becoming
a model

Ask the night manager if he'd ever thought of becoming
a model

Sleep five to a room and when discovered claim that
your guests are Equity members auditioning for a
musical

Claim, at the Ritz, that Lord Matthews is a personal
friend of yours

Ask for a room without a bath at Claridges

Ask for second helping in restaurant

Insist on visiting kitchen to congratulate chef

Carry own luggage to room

Book in as Mr and Mrs Smith

Exercise dog in corridor

Sodomise the boots

NAFF PUBS

The French Pub (Soho no-hopers)

El Vino's (too many journalists, not enough women)

The Salisbury (too many self-advertising theatrical
ninnies)

Finch's, The Fulham Road

The Water Rat, King's Road (too many villains)

The Admiral Codrington (too many merchant
bankers)

The Grenadier (too many whinnying guardsmen)

The Australian (too many Canadians)

The Boltons (too many Irish benders)

The Coach and Horses (too many sneaks and poets)

NAFF DRINKS

Piña colada
Lager and lime
Port and lemon
Mateus rosé
Cyprus sherry
Bacardi and Coke
Scotch and ginger
Vodka and orange
Crème de menthe
Avocaat
Babycham
Barbican

15
SEATS OF LEARNING

NAFF SCHOOLS

Felsted
Mill Hill
Millfield
Malvern
Clifton
Dover
Bloxham
Cranley
Harrow
Giggleswick
Stowe
Wellington
Haberdashers Aske's
Holland Park Comprehensive

NAFF THINGS SCHOOLMASTERS SAY

'I'm waiting . . .'
'It just isn't good enough'
'Take that expression off your face'
'A word in your shell-like ear . . .'
'Right you boys . . . when I blow the whistle . . . jump
on me!'
'I'm the ball. Scrum down!'

NAFF THINGS SCHOOLMASTERS DO

Superfluous *tinea cruris* inspections
Invite favoured boys for two weeks in Venice
Take extra swimming
Pull hair, ears, etc.
Buzz chalk, grind chalk into top of head
Drop the soap into schoolboy's bath and rummage for it
between adolescent thighs
Make you sit on their knee, feel their biceps etc.

NAFF EX-SCHOOLMASTERS

Russell Harty
Arthur Marshall
John Wells
Tom O'Connor (see *Naff Comedians*)
Anthony Chenevix-Trench
T. E. B. Howarth
Mary Parkinson

NAFF OLD WYKEHAMISTS

Peter Jay
Reginald Bosanquet
William Whitelaw
Sir Geoffrey Howe
Ian Gow
Ian Sproat
Douglas Jardine
Tim Brooke-Taylor
Alan Clark MP (not an Old Wykehamist but a silly ass
for all that)

NAFF NUMBER OF 'O' LEVELS

3
17 (suggests you must have been in prison)

NAFF NUMBER OF 'A' LEVELS

1 (History of Art)

NAFF EXAMINATIONS TO FAIL

Common Entrance
Oxbridge Entrance
Driving test (unless over 40 times)
Scripture 'O' level
Use of English

Sandhurst Entrance
Tinea cruris inspection (see *Naff Things School Masters Do*)
Police Sergeant's exam
Bar finals
Eng. Lit. BA
Army Medical

NAFF UNIVERSITIES

All naff except Oxford, Cambridge and the London School of Economics
The University of Real Life is especially naff (see *Naff Degrees*)

NAFF COLLEGES AT OXFORD AND CAMBRIDGE

OXFORD

Keble
St Catherine's
St Peter's Hall
Lincoln
Merton
Mansfield

CAMBRIDGE

Downing
Emmanuel
Selwyn
Jesus

NAFF DEGREES

Third in PPE at Oxford
2.2 in Eng. Lit. at Cambridge
History of Art at Open University
Honorary Degree in Engineering at the University of Lima (see Duke of Edinburgh)

Estate Management at Reading
Hotels, Catering and Tourism at Surrey
History of Drama at Bristol
A First in the University of Life (see Norman Tebbit)
Aegrotat in Divinity from Selwyn, Cambridge (esp. if
posthumously awarded – see God's Mysterious Ways
and *Naff Philosophical Theories*)

NAFF THINGS UNDERGRADUATES DO

Act out *Brideshead Revisited*
Assume names
Go down without a degree (see *Naff Boasts*)
Start new little magazines
Attend interview for job with Metal Box or Ogilvy,
Benson and Mather
Achieve office in the JCR
Get recruited by the KGB
Dress facetiously (esp. wing collars, pop waistcoats,
spongebag trousers, Beardsley bowties, Ulster coats,
etc.)
Stupefy themselves with debt, drink, drugs, etc.
Read Estate Management, Theology, Oriental Studies
Drive cars
Punt
Fall hopelessly in love
Impose images on others
Sit in
Write plays, novels, poems
Commit pre-finals suicide
Mount 'Tamburlaine The Great' in Salvation Army hut
at Edinburgh Festival
Make floor speeches at the Union
Have bricks thrown at them by street hooligans
Chant 'House! House! House!' in Eights Week
Bring arch little revues to London
Become actors
Put chamber pots on top of churches
Submit articles to *Punch*

16
LEISURE ACTIVITIES

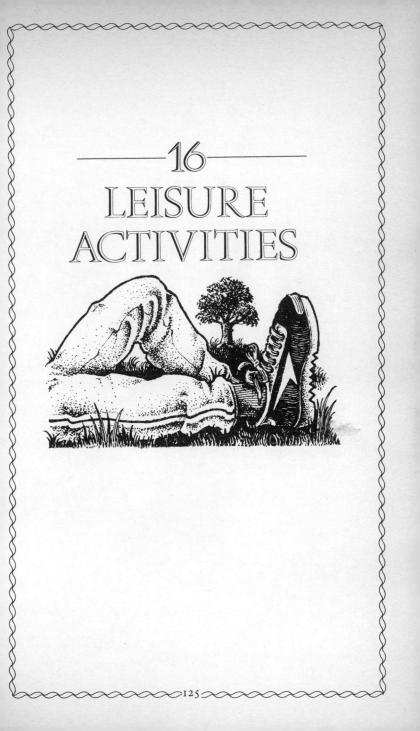

NAFF THINGS LONELY PEOPLE DO

Put lonely hearts ad in *Time Out*
Enrol with Computer Dating Service
Keep fit. Meditate. Jog. Stand on head
Watch 'Afternoon Plus'
Listen to the wireless
Go to dancing class
Put invitations on chimney-piece
Send Valentine cards
Join Tenants' Association
Learn Spanish
Go to a singles bar
Go on a singles holiday
Put up last year's Christmas cards
Do the *Standard* crossword
Put a humorous announcement on their answering
machine (see Peter Cook)
Leave humorous messages on other peoples' answering
machines (see *Naff Humorous Messages To Leave On
Other Peoples' Answering Machines*)
Visit call–girls just to talk
Join an amateur dramatic society
Read gossip columns (esp. Nigel Dempster)
Attend free lectures
Become a theatrical investor to meet girls
Go to art classes to see naked girls
Go into politics
Live with sister
Marry each other
Sleep rough, go mad, growl at women in the street
Write insane letters to the *Daily Express*

NAFF HUMOROUS MESSAGES TO LEAVE ON OTHER PEOPLES' ANSWERING MACHINES

Beep beep! 'How do you bring up a child in Australia?'
Beep beep! 'Stick your finger down a dingo's throat!'

Beep beep! 'What do you call a dog with wings?'
Beep beep! 'Linda McCartney!'

Beep beep! 'What does Dudley Moore do to Susan Anton?'
Beep beep! 'He goes *up* on her!'

NAFF THINGS TO DO AFTER THE AGE OF FORTY

HIM

Enter a 'Mr Thong Contest' on a package-tour holiday
Play organised football in Hyde Park
Learn to drive
Join a wife-swapping club
Enrol in the Open University
Write first novel
Become a mini-cab driver to finance writing of first novel
Move to a Mediterranean island to discover who you really are
Become gay
Be blackmailed by a male prostitute
Edit *Private Eye*
Learn to play the saxaphone
Wear pink socks
Visit unisex sauna baths
Become a prep-school master
Run with the bulls in Pamplona
Be made redundant
Be sent to prison for first time
Wear Walkman headphones

Start smoking marijuana
Buy clothes at Take Six
Make a TV series in Australia
Attend discotheques in shirt slit to the navel
Drive a sports car
Become player manager of Port Vale
Captain Yorkshire at cricket

HER

Wear a kanga
Have children
Appear as a principal boy in a pantomime (see Esther
Rantzen and *Naff Para-Sexual activities*)
Go on the game
Appear topless
Make porno movies in Rome
Buy clothes at Liberated Lady

NAFF THINGS TO DO UNDER THE AGE OF FORTY

Join the RAC
Play bridge
Move to the suburbs
Become an alcoholic
Have yearly medicals
Have three sons down for Eton
Emigrate to Canada
Become a Catholic
Commit suicide
Live in Somerset
Read the *Spectator*
Read the *Sunday Express*
Read the *Mail On Sunday*
Consider P. G. Wodehouse the greatest English writer
since Shakespeare
Vote Conservative
Pay for sex

Enrol with N.V.A.L.A.
Have an account at Truslove and Hanson
Make jokes about Channel 4, sociologists, polytechnic
teachers etc.
Take holidays in Scotland
Join a pension scheme
Drive a Volvo
Make excuses for Arthur Marshall
Refer to Malcolm Muggeridge affectionately as 'the
old boy'
Wear plus-fours

NAFF PASTIMES

Radio controlled boats in Kensington Gardens
Kite flying on Hampstead Heath
Fishing in a canal
Attending free lectures
Attending EST course
Collecting foil for PDSA
Skating at Queensway
Playing snooker at the RAC
Hanging around betting shops (see Jeffrey Bernard)
Plane-spotting
Pigeon racing
Radio controlled planes
CB radio
DIY
Making your own beer
Playing war games with toy soldiers
Ten-pin bowling
Jogging
Collecting stamps
Collecting autographs
Pressing flowers
Parachute jumping

Attending transactional analysis groups
Gourmandising
Karate (see Taki)
Cooking

NAFF THINGS TO SEE IN THE PORTOBELLO ROAD ON A SATURDAY MORNING

Community policemen hand-jiving with cheery
coloured gentlemen
Fat girls in ra-ra skirts
Men weeping
Actresses with barrows selling second editions
Mad old women singing 'Roses of Picardy'
Esther Rantzen asking vulgar and impertinent questions
Shit-faced German tourists
Bashed old-folk in doorways

NAFF GAMES

Scrabble
Backgammon
Roulette
Poker
Deck quoits
Clock golf
Crazy golf
'Diplomacy'
Space invaders
Newspaper casino
Chicken
Treasure hunts (esp. in the *Spectator*)
Truth, dare, kiss or promise
Bicycle polo (see Nigel Dempster)
Pass the orange
Matchbox nose to nose

NAFF DRUG SLANG

Stuff
Gear
Horse
Shit
Pot
Happy dust
Snow
Mary Jane
Wccd
California sunshine
Snort
Tipple
Plonk
One for the road
Tincture
A drop of medicinal
Bubbly

NAFF THINGS TO DO ON WIMBLEDON COMMON

Bash queers
Bash Wombles
Lose your virginity

NAFF LISTS

All lists submitted to Godfrey Smith by silly
schoolmasters with nothing better to do (esp. 'The Ten
Most Agreeable Dinner Companions Of All Time',
'The Ten Most Unforgettable Characters In Dickens',
'The Ten Tunes With The Top TQ' and 'The Ten Most
Delicious Words In The English Language').
All books of lists (esp. *The Book of British Lists*)
Shopping lists
Taki's hit-list

Michael Parkinson's Ten Favourite Ladies List:

1. Miss Piggy – the sexiest bit of cloth I ever seduced.
2. Catherine Bramwell-Booth – the great-granddaughter of the founder of the Salvation Army. She proves my theory that old people are the most interesting and the most honest to talk to.
3. Dame Edith Evans – for the same reason.
4. Diana Rigg – she disproves the theory that all actresses are dim. She's bright, on any topic.
5. Glenda Jackson – another intelligent actress.
6. Shirley MacLaine – it was one of my boyhood fantasies to run off with an American filmstar, a wise-cracking leggy broad from New York. I still fancy her.
7. Margot Fonteyn – for a lady of middle years, she's astonishing. She's like a young girl.
8. Bette Midler – another American star who's even more outrageous.
9. Erin Pizzey – she's a very articulate lady, and I approve of what she stands for.
10. The Wife. No, not because she'll read this but because I honestly think she's the best woman performer on TV. If she didn't have my name, she could be huge. She's a very good interviewer and she looks terrific.

Joan Collins's Ten Most Charismatic British Men:

1. Paul McCartney – has a little boy quality; is very together as a person and is one of the world's prolific songwriters.
2. Mick Jagger – raunchy, sexy, outrageous, eats up the stage as a performer; interesting off-stage.
3. Albert Finney – brilliant British stage actor; devastating, charming and fun in real life.
4. Prince Andrew – has the potential to outdo Prince Charles in the charm and daring stakes!
5. Lord Goodman – great presence and versatility, humorous, with an agile mind; he would have been a great politician.
6. 'Tiny' Rowland – the word 'impossible' is not in his vocabulary.
7. David Niven – the most debonair and gentlemanly English actor. He has the quality of making you feel that when you're with him you are the only person in the world he wants to be with. Also a great raconteur.
8. Sean Connery – a truly masculine man, he gets better as he gets older. Does not mind about ageing or going bald and as a consequence is more attractive.
9. Enoch Powell – politically speaking not my cup of tea but he is an evocative, fascinating speaker.

10. Kermit the Frog – has mass appeal and is liked by children, women and men. Cheeky and outrageous, although not handsome.

The *Daily Telegraph* readers' list of The Top Ten British Intellects Of This Century:

1. Winston Churchill.
2. Isaiah Berlin.
3. Evelyn Waugh.
4. Enoch Powell.
5. John Sparrow.
6. A. L. Rowse.
7. Aldous Huxley.
8. Margaret Thatcher.
9. Dr Julius Bronowski.
10. Bertrand Russell.

NAFF PRESENTS

Coat hangers

A subscription for *Cosmo*

A box of Cadburys Milk Tray

A copy of your latest book

Soap

Socks

The Guinness Book Of Records

Money (except family)

Electric plugs

An ice–container shaped like a pineapple

A gift voucher for Gilda shops

The Country Diary Of An Edwardian Lady

A box of drawer liners delicately perfumed with Woods of Windsor fragrance for gentlemen

A detachable keyring from Boots

A miniature Bonsai tree

A Boots body brush

An oven–glove shaped like a crocodile's head

A pink cotton padded tea cosy shaped like a pig

A set of *Country Diary* saucepans

The Lawn Expert

The Sex Maniac's Diary

─17─
NINE TO FIVE

Naff Jobs

PR
Process server
Policeman
Journalist
Prison warder
Male model
Minicab driver
Store detective
Newsreader (unless female)
Commodity broker (esp. if you have a degree)
Literary Editor of the *Sunday Express*

Naff Places to Advertise Your Services

Notice-board in newsagent's window
Taxi
Gay News (see *Naff Personal Behaviour*)
Telephone kiosk
Exchange and Mart
Private Eye (esp. humorous)

Naff Part-Time Jobs for Models

Call-girl
Hat-check girl at the Alibi Club
Bunny
Croupier
Shoplifter (esp. if Australian and male)

NAFF THINGS FOR MODELS TO DO

Sit on a Vauxhall topless at the Motor Show
Have a sex-change
Promote cigarettes at a tennis tournament
Be big in Japan
Be a Star Bird

NAFF BOYFRIENDS FOR MODELS

Record producer
Arms dealer
Arab prince
Car dealer
Villain
Stuntman
Jeans manufacturer
Karate expert
Airline co-pilot
Accountant (naff for a model or an actress to have an
accountant as a boyfriend, but not naff for secretaries,
bus conductresses or beauticians)

─18─
THE SPORTING LIFE

NAFF SPORTS

Wrist wrestling
Motor cross
Caber tossing
Darts
Rounders
Clay pigeon shooting
Badminton
Bicycling
French cricket
Pro/celebrity anything, esp. snooker
Cornish cock-fighting
Cockroach-racing
The dogs
Coursing
Hop, skip and jump
Putting the shot (for women)
Love doubles (see *Naff Couples*)
The London marathon

NAFF POSITIONS ON THE CRICKET FIELD

Mid-on

NAFF POSITIONS IN THE BATTING ORDER

7

NAFF CRICKET COUNTIES

Glamorgan
Derbyshire

NAFF WAYS OF GETTING OUT

Hit-wicket (esp. cap falling on stumps ducking a slow bumper)
Caught at mid-on off a slow full-toss from Eddie Hemmings
Caught at third-man trying to hook a good length ball
Run out on Boycott's call
Play for South African Breweries XI

NAFF TENNIS PLAYERS

Buster Mottram (super-naff)
Jimmy Connors (see *Naff Things Jimmy Connors Does*)
John McEnroe (see *Naff Fathers And Sons*)
All women tennis players are naff except Hana Mandlikova

NAFF THINGS JIMMY CONNERS DOES

Boasts
Grunts
Never gives up
Reads inspirational letters from mother at change-over between games
Makes obscene thrusting gesture with crutch on winning a point
Attempts infantile humour with crowd, opponent, linesmen, umpire, etc.

NAFF FOOTBALL CLUBS

Leeds United

NAFF GOALKEEPERS

Dai Davies of Swansea (has to take his teeth out before
the whistle goes)
Grobbelaar of Liverpool (see *Naff Names*)

NAFF FOOTBALLERS

All footballers are naff except Colin Todd of
Nottingham Forest

FOOTBALLERS WITH NAFF SQUEAKY VOICES

Alan Ball
Emlyn Hughes
Archie Gemmill

NAFF FOOTBALL MANAGERS

Ron Atkinson (see *Naff Hairstyles*)
John Bond (see *Naff Fathers And Sons*)
Brian Clough
Peter Taylor
Malcolm Allison (paradoxically not Tommy Docherty)

NAFF THINGS FOOTBALL MANAGERS SAY

'The wife and kids come first, Brian'
'All credit to the lads, Brian'
'It's a funny game football, Brian'
'It's all about good habits, attack, defence and winning
the midfield'

NAFF THINGS FOOTBALL MANAGERS SAY

'It was a real sickener when Forest scored that soft goal just before half-time, Brian. I saw my lads' heads go down'

'It was the little Argentinian that was the difference, Brian. You'd think he had radar in his boots. You can't legislate against skill like that'

'Of course I'd like to use a winger, Brian, a nippy little chap to get to the byeline and stick the ball onto the head of the big lad in the no. 9 shirt, but where am I going to find him? You tell me'

'We're not just going to Wembley to make up the numbers, Brian. Liverpool are going to know they've been in a match'

'We'll take each game as it comes, Brian. I'm making no predictions'

'That's the mark of a championship side, Brian. They still win when they're playing badly'

'This is a democracy, Brian. Just because we beat Liverpool one none at the City Ground we'd be stupid to think they're going to stuff us one none at Anfield. And we're not stupid here at Notts Forest, Brian'

'I don't care if the lad's black, brown, blue or purple with green spots, Brian. Just so long as he sticks the ball in the back of the net on Saturday I'll be well pleased'

RUGGER PLAYERS WITH NAFF NOSES

Graham Mourie
Roger Uttley

NON-RUGGER PLAYERS WITH NAFF NOSES

Barry Manilow
Russell Harty

Karl Malden
Tycho Brahe (paradoxically, a patient observer of
the heavens)
Orson Welles
Jimmy Durante
Diana Quick
Anthony Howard
Lewis Collins
Susan Hampshire
Princess Anne (paradoxically, not Barbra Streisand)
Dudley Sutton

NAFF SNOOKER PLAYERS WITH RED HAIR

Steve Davis

NAFF CHESS PLAYERS

There are no naff chess players (except in
The Seventh Seal)

NAFF WRESTLING HOLDS

The cross-buttock
The face-squat
The up-and-under
The sudden removal of the other fellow's trousers
The scrotum-grip

NAFF MISCELLANEOUS SPORTSMEN

Colin Cowdrey (see *Naff Divorces*)
Geoffrey Boycott (see *Candidates For The All-Time
Naffest Parkinson Show*)

NAFF MISCELLANEOUS SPORTSMEN

John Conteh
Joe Bugner
Geoff Capes
Harvey Smith (see *Naff Fathers And Sons*)
All darts players (esp. Eric Bristow)
Dennis Lillee
Rodney Marsh
All Australian cricketers (paradoxically, Australian
tennis players are among the least naff of their kind)
Kevin Keegan
Alan Ball
Emlyn Hughes
Ian Botham
Sebastian Coe
Mark Phillips

─19─
WELL-KNOWN
FACES

NAFF FOLK-HEROES

Billy Beaumont
Henry Cooper
Clare Francis
Fred Trueman
Lord Denning
Bobby Charlton
Brian Clough
Lord Grade
Enoch Powell
Geoffrey Boycott
Reggie Bosanquet (see *Naff Heterosexuals*)
'Tiny' Rowland
Jackie Stewart
James Cameron
Sefton

NAFF EX-PERSONALITIES

Sabrina
Bill Grundy
Tiny Tim
MacDonald Hobley
'Oxo' Katie
Hughie Green
Simon Dee
Bernard Braden
Barbara Kelly
Tariq Ali
Lady Docker
Princess Margaret
Screaming Lord Sutch
George Best
The Galloping Gourmet
Bianca Jagger
Peter Cook

NAFF EX-PERSONALITIES

Fanny Craddock
Viviane Ventura
Angela Bowie
Shirley-Anne Field
John Bloom
The Duchess of Argyll
Chris Tarrant
Eva Gabor
Emperor Roscoe
Mynah Bird
John Bentley
Katie Boyle
Jonathan King
Gyles Brandreth
Robert Dougall
P. J. Proby

NAFF THINGS PEOPLE SAY ABOUT MARILYN MONROE

She represented freedom to others but she wasn't free herself
She was sacrificed on the altar of our fantasies

NAFF FACES

Colin Welland
Mel Smith
Linda Lee-Potter
Elaine Page

NAFF EYEBROWS

Denis Healey
Gemma Craven
Meriel and Margaux Hemingway

NAFF BEARDS

Steve Race
Jimmy Hill
David Bellamy
Andrew Faulds

NAFF MOUSTACHES

Hitler
Raymond Glendenning

NAFF HAIRSTYLES

Sir Richard Attenborough
Dusty Springfield
Art Garfunkel (paradoxically, a good actor)
Bobby Charlton
Richard O'Brien
Mel Smith
Telly Savalas (paradoxically, not Yul Brynner)
Dolly Parton
Jan Leeming
Noel Edmonds
Charles Wheeler
Michael Heseltine
The Media Blowjob (see Barry Norman, Michael
Parkinson, etc.)
The Football Manager Parting Fractionally North Of
The Waist (see Ron Atkinson)
The lower–middle-class Racing Tadpole (see Sir Robert
Mark)
Bo Derek dreadlocks (unless non–Caucasian)
The Viscount Weymouth Silly Ass Plait
Mohawked
Glued hooligan

NAFF HAIRDRESSERS

Vidal Sassoon
Gavin Hodge
Rikki Burns
Dominick & Tony – Unisex Hairdressers. Raul Paul
and Dominick. The professionals in demi-wave and
blow-dry. Specialists in leg-waxing
Edward at the Churchill
John Frieda (see *Naff Couples*)
Lewis Collins
Delilah (see *Naff Biblical Characters*)

NAFF COUPLES

Paula Yates and Bob Geldorf
Hans and Lotte Hass
Erin Pizzey and Jeff Shapiro
Eric and Julia Morley
Nanette Newman and Bryan Forbes
Michael and Mary Parkinson (good old Parky)
Patrick Mower and Suzanne Danielle
Nigel Dempster and Lady Camilla
Little and Large
April Ashley and Duncan Fallowell
Armand and Michela Denis
Norman Scott and Jeremy Thorpe
Anna Raeburn and Nigel Lillie
Dorita y Pepé
Fanny and Johnny Craddock
Johnny and Raine Spencer
Cliff Richard and Sue Barker
Princess Anne and Mark Phillips
Joe and Marlene Bugner
John Frieda and Lulu
Barbara Windsor and Ronnie Knight

Victor Lownes and Marilyn Coles
Gilbert Lloyd and Emma Soames
Cliff Michelmore and Jean Metcalfe
Esther Rantzen and Desmond Wilcox
Louis Brown and Anthea Redfern
Bruce Forsyth and Wilnelia Merced
Annette Walter-Lax and Gareth Hunt (see *Naff Actors*)
Nina and Frederick
Anne and Pip Jones
Richard West and Mary Kenny
Tony Hatch and Jackie Trent
Liza Minelli and Peter Sellers
Jimmy Connors and Marjorie Wallace
Judi Dench and Michael Williams (see *Naff Sit-Coms*)
Dr Richard Arnot and Penny
Barry Sheen and Stephanie McLaine
Sue Lloyd and Ronald Allen
Chuck Traynor and Marilyn Chambers
Phillip Hodson and Anne Hooper
Larry Grayson and Noele Gordon
Noele Gordon and Val Parnell (see *Naff Kiss-Off Presents*)
Harbottle and Lewis (see *Naff Solicitors*)
Winston Churchill MP and Soraya Khashoggi
David and Elizabeth Emanuel
Lionel and Joyce Blair
Jackie Kimberley and Roxanne Pulitzer (see *Naff Divorces*)
Oliver Reed and Josephine Burge
Robert Runcie and Rosalind
Baron Steven Bentinck and Ingrid Seward
Diana Dors and Alan Lake
Ian McDonald and his mother
Rosie Swale and Tracey the sex-change
Hart and Hart

NAFF LOVE AFFAIRS

Jack Jones and Susan George
Pat Phoenix and Anthony Booth
Jeffrey Archer

NAFF DIVORCES

The Duke and Duchess of Argyll
Colin and Penny Cowdrey
John Lennon and Cynthia
Ringo Starr and Maureen
Pierre Trudeau and Margaret
Johnny and Frances Althorp
Joanna Lumley and Jeremy Lloyd
Rod Stewart and Britt Ekland
David Frost and Lynn Frederick
Harold Pinter and Vivian Merchant
Peter Pulitzer and Roxanne
Sir Hugh Fraser and Lady Antonia
Bruce Forsyth and Penny
All Elizabeth Taylor's
All Peter Sellers's
Richard Burton and Sybil

NAFF AUSTRALIAN ARRIVISTES

Rupert Murdoch
Kerry Packer
Lady Tryon
Nigel Dempster
Clive James
Robert Stigwood

NAFF NON-AUSTRALIAN ARRIVISTES

Taki
Robert Maxwell
Sir Michael Edwards
Tony Greig
Sir Charles Forte
Andre Deutsch
Victor Malik
Princess Michael of Kent
Sir James Goldsmith
Sir David English

NAFF DUTCH ARRIVISTES

Peregrine Worsthorne

NAFF MITFORDS

Unity
Debo
Diana

NAFF NANCIES

Nancy Sinatra
Nancy Reagan
Nancy Spain
Nancy Walker
Nancy Spurgeon
Kenneth Williams

NAFF DEAD BENDERS

Lord Bradwell
Godfrey Wynn
David and Jonathan (see *Naff Biblical Characters*)

NAFF MEMBERS OF 'BEYOND THE FRINGE'

Peter Cook
Dudley Moore

NAFF GROUPIES

Margaret Trudeau
Soraya Khashoggi
Francoise Pascal
Mynah Bird
Clive James

CAUSES OF NAFFNESS IN OTHERS
(see *Naff Lee-Potterisms*)

The Queen Mother (see *Naff Things People Say
About Royalty*)
Colonel H's widow
Ingrid Bergman
Grace Kelly
Mother Theresa
P.C. Olds
P. G. Wodehouse (see *Naff Things Metropolitan
Critics Say*)
Marilyn Monroe
Judy Garland
Dead hostesses (see *Naff Things Journalists Do*)

20
BEYOND THE CLOISTERS

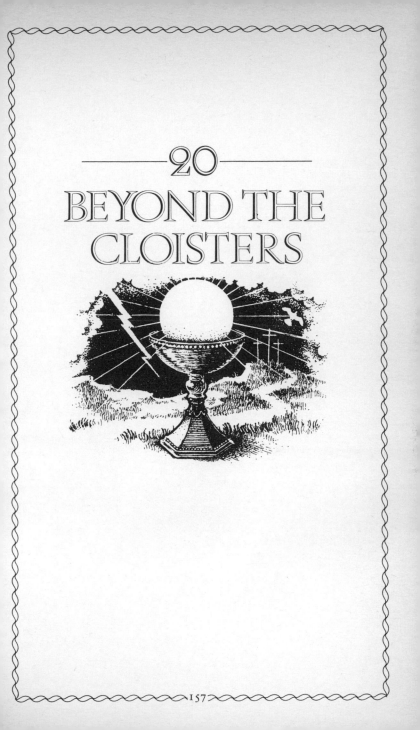

NAFF BIBLICAL CHARACTERS

Onan
Lot
Herod
The thief who wasn't saved
The prodigal son's father
Doubting Thomas
Goliath
Pontius Pilate
Esau
Delilah (see *Naff Hairdressers*)
Joseph's brothers
Joseph (cocky little bumsucker)
The centurian
The Samaritans
The Pharisees
The Philistines
The Hittites
Eve
David and Jonathan (see *Naff Dead Benders*)

NAFF SAINTS

St Pancras
St Michael
St Mugg

NAFF RELIGIOUS CONVERSIONS

Cat Stevens
Cassius Clay
Bob Dylan
Malcolm Muggeridge
St Paul
Cliff Richard

NAFF ANNOUNCEMENTS ON BECOMING A ROMAN CATHOLIC

'I have for many years been brooding over becoming a Catholic, but have been mysteriously held back. I even resisted the pleadings of Mother Theresa of Calcutta to join the church. What changed my mind was the Catholic Church's clear stand on such issues as contraception, abortion and euthanasia. This greatly appealed to me. Once I had decided to become a Catholic I felt a sense of homecoming, of picking up the threads of a lost life, of responding to a bell that had long been ringing, of finding a place at a table that has long been vacant.'

Malcolm Muggeridge

NAFF RELIGIONS

All religions are naff except the Church of England, which, with a few exceptions (see Dr Edward Norman and *Naff High Table Theologians*) requires no belief in God or other spooky superstitions about things that go bump in the night.

—21—
CALL TO ARMS

NAFF ARMIES

Egyptian
Salvation
Spanish
Territorial
Iraqi
French
Argentinian
United States
The stage-army of unrepresentative activists (see *Naff
Peregrine Worsthorne Expressions*)

NAFF REGIMENTS

3 Para
The Royal Engineers
The Skins
The Blues and Royals
The Gay Gordons

NAFF RANKS

Major
Lance-Corporal
Warrant Officer
Lieutenant-Commander
Surgeon-Lieutenant

NAFF WARS

Any Afghan
The Boer
The Korean
The Cod
The War of Jenkins's Ear
The Falklands

NAFF WARS

The Crimean
The Six Day (too short)
The Hundred Years (too long)

NAFF CAMPAIGNS

The Ethiopian
Buy British
Keep Britain Tidy
Save water – share a bath
Bring back the rope
The campaign for real ale
Small is beautiful
Moral rearmament
More means worse (see *Naff Jazz Buffs*)
A fair deal for stoats
Rock against racism
The Angry Women of Great Britain Against Sex-shops
Use it or lose it
Bombs before jobs
Home rule for Wales
Friends of the red squirrel
Norman Tebbit for Home Secretary
Jeremy Isaacs Must Go (see *Naff Things People Say
About Channel 4*)
Shoppers against Sunday Shopping

22
FAMILY LIFE

NAFF CHILDREN

Winston Churchill MP
Paul Grade
Princess Caroline of Monaco
Timothy Sainsbury
Patty Hearst
Sir Rupert Mackeson
Baron Steven Bentinck
Julian Lennon
Michael and Sarah Sellers
Val Lownes
Piers Shore
Charlie Tennant
Jamie Blandford
Brezhnev's boy
Ronnie Reagan Jnr
Lynn Frederick
Patrick Wayne
Frank Sinatra Jr
Paul Getty II
Amy Carter
Mark Thatcher
Taki
Sir William Rees-Mogg's brat
Bobby Butlin

NAFF BROTHERS

Roddy and Dai Llewellyn
Norris and Ross McWhirter
Charlie and Eddie Richardson
The Nash brothers
Bernard and Anthony Shrimsley
Paul and Barry Ryan
Greg, Ian and Trevor Chapple
John and Roy Boulting

NAFF BROTHERS

Cec and Dec Clusky
The Bee Gees (see *Naff Bee Gees*)
Moss Bros
Lord Grade and Lord Delfont
Rodney and Graham Marsh
Alan and Chris Old
Bob and Alf Pearson
John and Sam Silkin
David and Donald Cammell

NAFF BROTHERS-IN-LAW

Alan Watkins and Anthony Howard

NAFF SONS-IN-LAW

Peter Jay

NAFF SISTERS

Joan and Jackie Collins
The Nolan Sisters (except Bernadette)
The Beverley Sisters (esp. Babs)
Jackie Onassis and Lee Radziwell
Vanessa and Lynn Redgrave

NAFF MOTHERS AND DAUGHTERS

Barbara Cartland and Raine Spencer
Molly Parkin and Buzz
Princess Elizabeth of Yugoslavia and Catherine
Oxenberg
Moira Lister and Chantal

NAFF FATHERS AND SONS

Mr McEnroe and John
Mr Coe and Seb
Papa Doc and Little Doc
John Bond and Kevin
Harvey Smith and Robert

NAFF FATHERS AND DAUGHTERS

Jess and Paula Yates
Lord Hailsham and Kathy Hogg
Richard Nixon and Pat Eisenhower
Sir John and Penny Junor
Jimmy Carter and Amy
Leonid Brezhnev and Galina
Hugh Hefner and Christine

NAFF MOTHERS AND SONS

Mrs Thatcher and Mark
Mrs Connors and Jimmy
Mrs Lillian Carter and Jimmy

23
THE BODY POLITIC

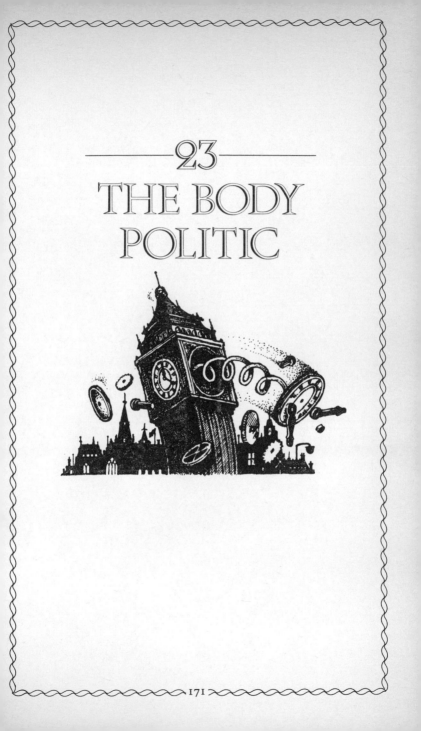

NAFF PEERS

Lord Wigg
Lord Lucan
Lord Rothermere
Lord Grade
Lord Delfont
Lord Hesketh
Lady Falkender
Lord Gormley
Lord Scanlon
Lord Matthews
Lord Kagan
Lord Warwick
Lord Hailsham
Lord Henry Herbert
The Duke of Devonshire
Lord Belper
Lord Montague of Beaulieu
Viscount Weymouth
The Duke of Bedford
Earl Jermyn
The Marquess of Bristol
Lord Moynihan
Lord Newport

NAFF TITLES

Miss Nude Europe
Welter-weight champion of Belgium
Chief Barker
Lord George-Brown
Mr Scotland
The Best Mum in The World (see *Naff Editorials*)

NAFF POLITICAL APPOINTMENTS

Postmaster General
Minister of Transport
Vice-president of the United States
Minister of Agriculture and Fisheries
Deputy Speaker
Minister of Arts in a Conservative government
President of the German Democratic Republic
Minister of Sport
Minister of Weather
Chairman of the Arts Council

NAFF POLITICIANS

FAT

Cyril Smith
Eric Heffer
Geoffrey Dickens
Hector Monroe

CONCEITED

Sir Nicholas Fairbairn
Neil Kinnock
Dr David Owen

FAT AND CONCEITED

Nigel Lawson
Leon Brittain
Roy Jenkins

THICK

Winston Churchill
Sir Nicholas Bonsor
Eldon Griffiths
Christopher Brocklebank-Fowler
John Corrie
Anthony Nelson

DEMENTED

Norman Tebbit
Teddy Taylor
Dr Rhodes Boyson
Sir Keith Joseph
Lord Hailsham
Enoch Powell
Alan Clark
George Gardiner
Frank Allaun

FAT AND DEMENTED

The Reverend Ian Paisley

FEMALE

Judith Hart
Joan Lestor
Sally Oppenheim

BOSSY OLD TROUTS

Margaret Thatcher
Miss Bluebell
Barbara Woodhouse (Miss Bluebell and Barbara Woodhouse aren't politicians but they are bossy old trouts)

NAFF THINGS MRS THATCHER SAYS

'The Lady's not for turning!'
'Rejoice!'
'The secret of happiness is to live within your income and pay your bills on time'

NAFF THINGS PEOPLE SAY ABOUT MRS THATCHER

Peregrine Worsthorne writes:
'As many have remarked of Mrs Thatcher's Falklands visit, her manner there was more regal than the Queen's. This was not electioneering: more a religious pilgrimage.

NAFF THINGS PEOPLE SAY ABOUT MRS THATCHER

Nothing wrong with that. The Falklands war did stir the nation's deepest feelings, as a result of which the Prime Minister is now a very special person, tinged with a kind of majesty.'

Jean Rook writes:

'Margaret Thatcher is now awesome. No longer just a national figure. She's inexorably turning into a bronze monument of herself. She is living out a legend in the Falklands which will go down in history.

Years after she and her politics have crumbled, they'll carve Magnificent Maggie's name with pride on statues from Grantham to Goose Green. And write it in red, blue and enviously green ink.

When Ronald Reagan calls her "the best man in Britain" he couldn't be more wrong – apart from her heart and stomach for the rough twenty-three-hour flight and the stamina of a marine.

Because only a woman has the emotional range to survive what Maggie has endured in three days which would have half-killed stronger men of half her age.

By "emotional" I don't mean an act. The Thatcher is no bombastic Benn or farcical back-sliding Foot.

She has stood as firm as she did through the 1982 war in the eye of a storm of passionate patriotism wild as the Falklands weather and let it sweep over her.

Maggie has done it for the Falklanders and done it magnificently. Not just the yomping through the minefields or the middle-aged tigress's trying on the Royal Hampshire "Tigers" T-shirt or the triggering off of the men's respect by firing a 105mm gun as only a woman can. But the endurance with which she has faced the sorrowing at the cemeteries in gratitude for the greater endurance and sacrifice of those who lost their lives to win Britain's fight.

A task force in herself since the moment she left the plane, she has proved herself not the "best man in Britain" but the Woman For All Seasons.

She has proved herself The Woman of Destiny. The exam-loving Grantham grocer's daughter turned chemist, turned barrister, who turned herself into not just the first British woman Prime Minister but foreseeably the most formidable in decades – if not centuries.

She combines a little of all that's best in British womanhood. The bravery of Boadicea. The dedication and compassion of Nightingale. The arrogance, especially towards wet men, of an Elizabeth I. And the stubbornness of an Emily Brontë insisting on feeding the cat just before she died sitting bolt upright on the end of a sofa.

Add a stony breath of the Gorgon if she's crossed and Margaret Thatcher is one hell of a terrifyingly prodigious woman.'

NAFF THINGS TO CALL MRS THATCHER

The Leaderene
The Blessed Margaret
Heather
Tina
Attila the Hen
The best man in the Cabinet
The best man in the country
A horse's arse

NAFF MAJORITIES

The Silent
The Moral
The Put-Upon
The Long-Suffering
The Vast Majority of Decent, *Moderate* Trade Union Members

NAFF GREAT LOST LEADERS

Rab Butler
Iain Macleod
Sir Oswald Mosley
Enoch Powell
Sir Robin Day
Jo Grimond
Bob Boothby

24

THE ARM OF
THE LAW

NAFF CRIMES

Stealing credit cards from fellow members in the
changing-room at Queen's Club
Cheating at 'Spot the Ball'
Sticking up postmistresses
Burglarising parents' friends
Fraudulent insurance claims
Defrauding mother
Drunken driving (see Mel Smith)
Spying on behalf of South Africa
Sex crimes (except running a brothel)
Drunk and disorderly (esp. if acquitted – see Reginald
Bosanquet)

NAFF CRIMINALS

'Mad' Frankie Fraser
The Flying Squad

NAFF THINGS TO CALL POLICEMEN

Rozzers
Pigs
The filth
The fuzz (paradoxically, not old Bill)
Inspector (if obviously a constable)
Sir

NAFF THINGS POLICEMEN SAY

'Right, Stirling Moss . . .'
'We've got a comedian here, have we? Right,
Bob Hope . . .'
'Don't be like that, John, you've been a naughty boy'
'You're well overdue for a pull, son'

NAFF THINGS POLICEMEN SAY

'Ho yes? And I'm the Queen of Sheba'
'You're a million to go in the frame, son'
'There'll be earners in this one, Ron'
'For a drink I could drop you out'
'And at that point, your honour, the accused assaulted me with his groin'

NAFF THINGS CHIEF POLICE OFFICERS SAY

'All police forces contain the odd bad apple and the Met's no exception'

NAFF POLICE OPERATIONS

Operation Swamp
The Balcombe Street Siege
The Spaghetti House Siege
Ambushing and shooting the wrong car in Pembroke Road
The arrest of Liddell Towers
The arrest of James Kelly
The hunt for the Yorkshire Ripper
The Luton Post Office murder investigation
The arrest of Ronnie Biggs
Vietnam 63–66
Toxteth 81

NAFF PROSECUTIONS

The Police v. Oz
Mary Whitehouse v. 'The Romans in Britain'
Mary Whitehouse v. *Gay News*
The Police v. Timothy Evans
The Police v. James Hanratty

The Police v. Tiddy Dolls Eating House
France v. Dreyfus
The police v. Lady Chatterley
The police v. Stephen Ward

NAFF COVER-UPS

Operation Countryman
Chappaquiddick
The shooting of the Argentine sailor in South Georgia
The killing of the Iranian terrorists by the SAS
Patrick Marnham's *The Private Eye Story – The First Twenty-One Years*
The Helen Smith inquest
The Fisher Report in the Confait killing
The Blair Peach inquest
The Deptford fire inquest
The death of Barry Prosser in Winson Green prison
The Denning Report after the Profumo scandal
The Franks Report
The shooting of Colin Roach
The New Cross Massacre
Sir David English's pitiful attempt to bamboozle the Press Council into believing that a) the *Daily Mail* had never bid for the Yorkshire Ripper's wife's story and b) when this was shown to be a lie, that it had only done so to up the price other papers would have to pay

NAFF REASONS FOR BEING AGAINST CAPITAL PUNISHMENT

It isn't practical
It makes juries reluctant to convict
It creates martyrs
Hanging the wrong man is rather final, but thirty years inside for something you didn't do never hurt anyone

NAFF JUDGES

Sir Melford Stevenson

Lord Justice Lawton – 'After thirty years on the bench I can smell a criminal'

Lord Dilhorne

Mr Justice Cantley – appeared for the defence at Jeremy Thorpe's trial

Mr Justice Boreham – unimpressed by so-called expert witnesses, it took him just five minutes to decide that the Yorkshire Ripper was not suffering from a mental disease but was in fact a perfectly normal man – a sadistic killer of, for the most part, innocent women

All crown court judges, esp. Judge King-Hamilton QC and Judge Buzzard QC – 'Justice must tame whom mercy fails to train'

The Common Sergeant, esp. Mervyn Griffith-Jones QC

All Miss World judges

NAFF KEY WITNESSES

Mr A, Mr B and Mr Y (the Janie Jones trial)

Joe Valachi

Commander Kenneth Drury

Peter Bessell (the Thorpe trial)

Dr Richard Arnot

Mandy Rice-Davies and Christine Keeler (the Stephen Ward trial)

Mary Whitehouse, always

'Mad' Frankie Fraser (character witness for Ronnie Kray)

NAFF SUPERGRASSES

Bertie Smalls

Ronnie 'the Weasel' Hart

Nigel Dempster

All reporters on the *News of the World*, but esp. Tina
Dalgliesh (as a woman she should know better)
Richard Ingrams
Ian Gow MP (special grass to Mrs Thatcher)
The 'That's Life' team
John Dean

NAFF EXCUSES

'I was only doing my job'

'I must have been drunk'

'She looked at least seventeen'

'The computer's broken'

'The cheque's in the post'

'It's the wrong time of the month'

'I value our friendship too much'

'You frightened him' – after you've been savaged by
your neighbour's doberman

After the shooting of Stephen Waldorf by the police,
the *Sunday Telegraph* writes:

'It is unreasonable to put blame on the police. The root of
the problem lies in criminal trigger-happiness, to which
the police must feel tempted to react for minimal self-
protection.'

'I'm sorry, Nigel, but I happen to be in love with my
husband. Is that frightfully boring of me?'

'The Belgrano was a threat to the Task Force'

NAFF SOLICITORS

Sir David Napley
Harbottle and Lewis
Oscar Beusalink
Adonis Kyriakides & Co.
Bindman and Partners
Boodle and King
Eric Levine and Co.
Rooks Rider and Co.

NAFF SOLICITORS

Sharp Bentley and Co.
Le Brasseur and Bury
Crossman, Block and Keith
Oswald Hickson, Collier and Co.

NAFF TO BE CAUGHT

Short
Napping
At the scene of the crime
With your hand in the till
On the hop
With your trousers down

25
ON THE
BOARDS

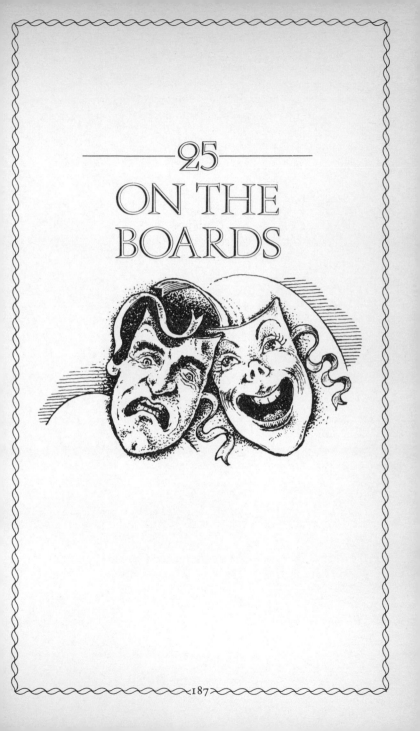

NAFF THINGS PEOPLE DO AT THE THEATRE

Eat chocolates
Talk
Take children
Explain plot to deaf aunt
Arrive late, leave early
Wear hats, bouffant hair
Cry 'Bravo!'
Cry 'Author!'
Snore
Go backstage in interval to congratulate cast
Shout 'Fire' (see *Naff Philosophical Theories*)
Laugh on cue having seen the play before
Laugh at sallies by Shakespearian Fools
Declaim well-known speech from Shakespeare along
with actors
Buy one programme between two or more people
Stand up to applaud
Leave during curtain calls
Participate, sing-along, clap in unison, etc.
Drink furtively from flask
Boo

NAFF THINGS PEOPLE DO AT A FRINGE THEATRE

Complain about seats
Complain about smell (see *Naff Smells*)
Complain about the play

NAFF QUOTES TO SEE OUTSIDE A THEATRE

'An evening of civilized humour'
'Bawdy fun!'

NAFF QUOTES TO SEE OUTSIDE A THEATRE

'Irreverent nonsense'
'Positively Rabelaisian'
'Felicity Kendal is a pure delight'
'Kenneth Williams at his most outrageous'
'An evening of quiet drollery . . . the impeccable Paul
Eddington . . . the incomparable Penelope Keith . . .
the audience roared!'

NAFF THINGS ACTORS DO ON STAGE

Corpse
Spray
Spit
Screech
Bellow
Die well
Go glassy
Shoot cuffs
Boom
Pose (see Barry Foster)
Run on stage instead of walk
Enter, close door behind them and lean against it
Wear enigmatic, pussycat smiles (see Diana Rigg,
Joanna Lumley and Gerald Harper)
Smirk irrepressibly (see Felicity Kendal)
Run skittishly towards leading man (see Susannah
York)
Address lines to ceiling, audience, outer space –
anywhere but in direction of opposing mime
Persistently leave mouth hanging open after delivery of
line (see Gerald Harper)
Cover weak line with Groucho Marx walk (see
Maureen Lipman) or Bogart voice

NAFF THINGS ACTORS DO OFF STAGE

Burst into tears
Stamp feet
Ask management to fire director
Complain to agent
Ask for day off to shoot porno movie
Sue Paul Raymond for publishing stills from porno
movie in *Men Only*
Appear nude because the integrity of script demands it
Shriek in restaurants
Touch each other
Project charm
Appear on 'Celebrity Knockout'
Appear as guests on 'The Morecambe and Wise Show'
Write children's books
Make enthusiastic fools of themselves in commercials
for the *Guardian* (see Susannah York)
Write memoirs under silly titles (*Up In The Clouds
Gentlemen Please*)
Tell rambling anecdotes on chat shows

NAFF ACTORS

Robin Askwith
Lewis Collins
Patrick Mower
Peter Bowles
Walter Gotell
Barry Foster
Stratford Johns
Derek Nimmo
William Marlowe
George Sewell
Nicky Henson
Robert Hardy
Gareth Hunt
Gerald Harper

NAFF ACTORS

Norman Bowler
Edward Woodward
Patrick Allen
Jack Watling
Guy Rolf
Simon Williams
Ian Ogilvie
Keith Barron
Paul Daneman
Edward de Souza
Leslie Crowther
Oliver Reed
Colin Baker
Richard Burton

NAFF AMERICAN ACTORS

Telly Savalas

NAFF ACTRESSES

Glenda Jackson
Susannah York
Wendy Craig
Nanette Newman
June Whitfield
Pat Phoenix (indeed, all actresses in Coronation Street
except 'Annie Walker' and 'Hilda Ogden')
Jill Gascoigne
Maureen Lipman
Joanna Lumley
Jean Marsh
Rita Tushingham
Julie Covington

Moira Lister
Barbara Murray
Noele Gordon

NAFF PART-TIME JOBS FOR ACTRESSES

Waitress
Work in a wine bar (paradoxically, it's not naff for
models to work in wine bars)
Stripper
Stooge on '3,2,1' or 'Sale Of The Century'
Char for Domestics Unlimited
Write TV plays or children's books
Do answering machine announcements for other people

NAFF THINGS FOR ACTRESSES TO DO

Sell old clothes from a stall in Portobello Road or
Camden Lock markets
Share audition clothes with another actress (worse to
share photographs or boyfriends, esp. if Arab prince)
Accept bookings in the Middle East

NAFF RECITATIONS

Edward Woodward reading from *Other Men's Flowers* in
Auckland, New Zealand
Susannah York reading fey excerpts from one of her
silly children's books on 'The Other Side Of Me'
Richard Burton reciting the present indicative of the
verb 'to be' on a chat show
Bonnie Langford reciting the Lord's Prayer on the
Epilogue
Anthony Andrews reading a letter from his mother on
receiving a best TV actor of the year award
John Alderton reading passages from P. G. Wodehouse
on BBC2

NAFF RECITATIONS

Michael Paul Glazer declaiming the Gettysburg Address
at the Oscar presentations

Barry Took reading excerpts from the immortal
Beachcomber anywhere

Diana Rigg reciting anything anywhere

Angela Rippon reciting Kipling's 'Recessional' at the
Royal Command Performance

Enoch Powell reciting his own early verses in the
Horatian mode on 'The Parkinson Show'

Moira Lister reading the sermon on the mount on 'Lift
Up Your Hearts'

Margaret Thatcher reciting 'Oh Valiant Hearts' beside
Colonel H's grave in the course of a party political
broadcast

NAFF SHAKESPEAREAN CHARACTERS

Horatio

Laertes

Trinculo

Quince

Pistol

John of Gaunt

Macduff

Chorus

NAFF MUSICALS

'Jesus Christ Superstar'

'Evita'

'Annie'

'Hullo Dolly'

'The Sound of Music'

'Twang'

'Mame'

'Camelot'

'Oliver'

'Charlie Girl'

NAFF IMPRESARIOS

All impresarios are naff except Michael Codron

NAFF OSCAR ACCEPTANCE SPEECHES

Lord Olivier (mock humble and unintelligible)
Colin Welland (boastful and common)
Jane Fonda (emetic daughterly love)
Vanessa Redgrave (insultingly half-witted)

NAFF SHOW FOLK

Escapologists
Dwarves
Conjurors
Clowns
Augustes
Old Time Music Hall Masters Of Ceremonies
Contortionists
Comic instrumentalists
Jugglers
Rolf Harris

NAFF NON-EQUITY MEMBERS

Daleks
Muppets
Captain Beaky
Lamp Chop
Flower Pot Men (but not little Weed)
Nooky
Muffin the Mule (see *Naff Sexual Practices*)
Wombles
Hercules the Bear
Jimmy Savile

NAFF DR WHOS

William Hartnell
The wet vet

NAFF PRODUCTS TO ENDORSE ON TV

Odour eaters
Dandruff shampoos
Denture cleaners and fixatives
Lavatory paper
The Conservative Party
Acne cleansers
The *Mail On Sunday*

26
THE WORLD
OF SONG

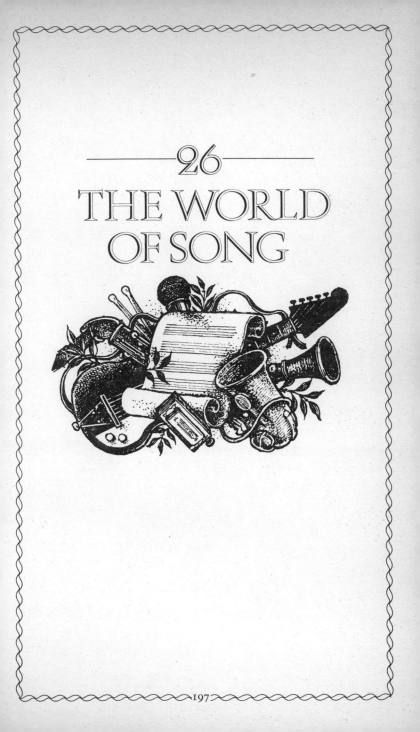

NAFF CONCERT PROGRAMMES

Tchaikovsky's '1812' overture
Greig's 'Peer Gynt Suite'
Ravel's 'Bolero'
Bach's 'Air on a G-string', arranged for strings
'Peter and the Wolf', narrated by Richard Baker

NAFF BALLET ROLES

Von Rothbart, the wicked owl in 'Swan Lake'
Dr Coppelius
Hilarion
The tutor who keeps falling over in 'Swan Lake'
The four stiffs in the Rose Adagio
The Ugly Sisters in 'Cinderella'
Carrabosse, the wicked rat in 'The Sleeping Beauty'
The naff little girl in 'The Nutcracker Suite'
The big girl's blouse in 'Les Sylphides'
The conceited ponce in 'Romeo and Juliet'

NAFF NON-SEQUITURS

The *Daily Express* writes:
'Ballet star Wayne Sleep, 32, has had a career lasting twenty years despite his five feet two-and-a-half inch frame.'

NAFF BEE GEES

Robin

NAFF WELSH SINGERS

Shirley Bassey
Tom Jones
Ivor Emmanuel

NAFF NON-WELSH SINGERS

Vince Hill
Matt Monro
Frankie Vaughan
Petula Clark
Lulu
Jack Jones
Sheena Easton
Barry Manilow
Englebert Humperdinck
Lena Zavaroni
Val Doonican
Howard Keel
Marti Caine
Cilla Black
Andy Stewart
Kenneth McKellar
Lena Martell
Dana
Elton John
John Denver
Glen Campbell

NAFF SINGING EX-NUNS

Mary O'Hara

NAFF GROUPS

Instant Sunshine
Demis Roussos
Abba
Bucks Fizz
The Nolan Sisters
The Osmonds
Kids International
Bing Crosby and David Bowie
Dino, Dezi and some berk (very well known in
America, but soon petered out)

NAFF SONGS
'As Long As He Needs Me'
'Moon River'
'Granada'
'My Boy Lollipop'
'Yesterday'
'Everyone's Gone To The Moon'
'Tell Laura I Love Her'
'Goldfinger'
'Bridge Over Troubled Water' (in Spanish)
'Congratulations'
'My Way'
Any song by Shirley Bassey
'Delilah' (see *Naff Hairdressers*)
'Pickin' a Chicken'
'The Green Green Grass Of Home'
'The Leader Of The Pack'
'Diana'
'Born Free'
'Don't Cry For Me Argentina'
'Tell Me On Sunday, Please'
'Love is Like A Violin'
'Jealousy'
'Imagine'
'Annie's Song'
Any song by the English World Cup Squad

NAFF DEAD POP STARS
Sid Vicious
Bing Crosby

NAFF THINGS LONELY POP STARS SAY
'I've just made love to 250,000 people and I'm going
home alone'

NAFF COLLABORATORS WITH TIM RICE
Andrew Lloyd-Webber

27
ON THE AIR

NAFF COMEDIANS

Lenny Henry
Jim Davidson
Dave Allen
Terry Scott
Ted Rogers
Kelly Monteith
Tom O'Connor
Jimmy Tarbuck
Dickie Henderson
Max Bygraves
Kenneth Williams
Leslie Crowther
John Inman
Cannon and Ball
Bernie Winters
Little and Large
Morecambe and Wise

NAFF RADIO PROGRAMMES

'Any Questions'
'Any Answers'
'Start the Week'
'Stop the Week'
'The Jimmy Young Show'
'Quote, Unquote'
'News Quiz'
'Midweek Theatre'
'Does He Take Sugar?'

THE ALL-TIME NAFFEST PAGE
IN THE *RADIO TIMES*

The 7.0 News on Radio 4. (Very naff to be up at this time)

7.50. 'It's A Bargain'. Norman Tozer with how to get the best from your hard-earned cash. Today: Paraffin heaters.

12.30. 'The Food Programme' – Have A Good Dinner, You Folks! Derek Cooper flies to California, sampling a hot meal over the cold ice-floes of Greenland and discovering why cabin crews never stop drinking. In the Napa Valley he's told it's chic to own a 'boutique' vineyard, meets an English couple running a 'gourmet diner' and receives strange messages from the tube!

4.10. 'Take 300 Swans . . .' The extravagances of Elizabethan entertaining inspire Roger Worsley to do a little research into the finer points of 16th century cuisine. The result is a banquet (without swans and with the merest six courses!) prepared according to the recipes of the day. His neighbours in Pembrokeshire are Wynford Vaughan-Thomas and Professor Brian Morris. Join him for the feast!

5.05. 'Down Your Way'. Brian Johnston visits Ilminster in Somerset. He discovers a quiet country town but with a surprising amount of industry, lots of associations with famous people, and a snuff-taking champion!

7.30. Hubert Gregg says 'I Call It Genius'. This week: Busby Berkeley.

9.00. 'Pleasures'. Nine talks by Bernard Levin. 6: Shakespeare. 'Shakespeare's mind is an instrument of such stupendous understanding, depth and creativity that it towers over the human race. And his poetry, in which he presented the contents of that mind, provides a pleasure that consumes like fire'. (Next talk: My agreeable eating holiday in the Dordogne.)

9.30. 'Stick a Geranium In Your Hat!' A celebration in four parts of the words and music of R. P. Weston and Bert Lee, starring Roy Hudd as Bob Weston and Billy Dainty as Bert Lee, with Ian Smith at the piano. 2. 'My word, you do look queer', devised and written by Roy Hudd.

11.00. 'Barry Took's Late Show'. Barry Took hosts an early-early breakfast show for the night before the morning after, with music, guests and good conversation

NAFF TV PROGRAMMES

'Call My Bluff'
'My Music'
'Face the Music'
'The Gentle Touch' (see *Naff Actresses*)
'Tales of the Unexpected'
All chat shows
'Around With Allis' (see *Naff Snug-bar philosophers*)
'Hart to Hart' (see *Naff Couples*)
'We'll Meet Again'
'That's Life'
'Name That Tune'
'The Monte Carlo Show'
All sit-coms are naff except those written by Peter Tinniswood and Roy Clarke
The Royal Command Performance (paradoxically not 'The Eurovision Song Contest' or 'Miss World')
'Afternoon Plus'
'Omnibus'
All game shows, esp. 'Game For A Laugh'

NAFF BARRY NORMAN EXPRESSIONS

'Some you win, some you lose'
'Meanwhile, back at the ranch'
'That can't be bad'
'D. H. Lawrence may have been a bit of a party-pooper, but he sure could write'
'And I quote'
'Right on!'
'Rubinstein he ain't, but the guy's got style'
'There's no answer to that'

NAFF CHARACTERS IN AMERICAN SOAP OPERAS

Chin in 'Hawaii Five-O'
Clive Barnes in 'Dallas'
Det Sapperstein in 'Kojak'
The cocky grass in 'Starsky and Hutch' (black)
Bum-face in 'Hart to Hart' (the cook who can't act)
Benson in 'Benson' (plus irritating little madam)
Macmillan's wife in 'Macmillan And Wife' (plus nosey cook)
Little Joe in 'Bonanza'

NAFF FRONT-PERSONS

Barry Norman
Tony Gubba
Miriam Stoppard
Barry Took
Harry Carpenter
Esther Rantzen
Clive James
Jimmy Hill
Michael Parkinson
David Vine
Russell Harty
Denis Nordern
Bob Topping
Steve Jones
The four giggling pin-heads on 'Game For A Laugh'

NAFF HANDICAPS FOR AMERICAN TV DETECTIVES

Baldness
Blindness

Fatness
Paraplegia
Stupidity
Inability to act

NAFF TV INTERVIEW QUESTIONS

'How did you feel when you:
Scored the winning goal?
Heard you'd had your legs off?
Were given the news that both your sons had been killed
in Northern Ireland?
Realised you'd won the Eurovision Song contest for
Sweden?'

'How long did it take you to write this book?'

'How closely is the leading character based on you?'

How do you answer those critics who've called it a piece
of infantile pornography?'

'Do you ever regret giving up medicine for the bright
lights of show business?'

'How does it feel to be a sex object?'

'When did you first discover that you could make
people laugh? Was it a defence mechanism against being
bullied at school?'

'You must have had some hilarious experiences making
twenty-five "Carry On" films. Tell us about them.'

'You've worked for, and known intimately, eight
Presidents of the United States, Professor. Which one,
in your opinion, most enjoyed a wisecrack?'

'Do you still get nervous before a performance, Sir
Ralph?'

'Why, Sir Freddie, should a great philosopher such as
yourself be interested in football?'

'It's been quite a year for you, Andrew. Your father fell
over dead and you've had three musicals in the West
End. Tell us about it.'

NAFF AWARDS

The *Standard* Most Promising Actor Award (see Nicky Henson)

The *TV Times* Personality of the Year

The 'Nationwide' Pop and Rock Awards

Thames TV Glamorous Granny Award

The 'What The Papers Say' Occasional Felicitous Endpiece Award (see Roy Hattersley)

The West Heath Service to Others and Best Kept Hamster Award (see Princess Diana)

The Woman Of The Year

The Lord Denning Golden Bull for Plain English (that even a sub on the *Daily Mail* could understand)

The *Cosmo* Young Journalist of the Year Award

The CBE

The *TV Times* £10 Letter of the Week to 'Dear Katie' Award

NAFF RIPOSTES

Paula Yates writes:

'Anyone remember Tony Blackburn? Well, the veteran DJ has really flipped his turntables over my new TV spectacular, "The Tube".

Touchy Tone reckons I shouldn't be allowed anywhere near a television camera. And he blew a fuse on Radio One over my Channel 4 pop-show.

Surprisingly Tone didn't object to my pregnant appearance, which I admit bore an uncanny resemblance to a pumped-up blancmange!

He just reckoned I'd no right to host the show when I've no telly experience.

Tone's wobbler delighted "The Tube" producer Malcolm Gerrie. "What a great plug for the show, kid!" he said.

And his outburst certainly didn't bother me. Anyone who has to resort to Arnold, a tape-recorded dog, for company can't really be taken seriously!'

NAFF THINGS PEOPLE SAY ABOUT CHANNEL 4

'Channel bore – that's what I call it'

'I can top you there – Channel four-letter word!'

James McMillan (see *Naff Journalists*) writes:
'The television programme "To The Manor Born" is a popular show because it appeals to two thoroughly British traits: class consciousness and a love of local gossip.

Poor Channel 4 is being ignored by viewers in droves because it spurns such things.

Instead Jeremy Isaacs, chief of Channel 4, seems obsessed with the problems of so-called "concerned" minorities: West Indians, homosexuals, Asians, the oppressed, the disadvantaged.

But we tune into television to be entertained. The minority watching Channel Swore may soon be composed of Jeremy Isaacs!'

Winston Churchill MP writes:
'What viewers want is good family entertainment, like you get every day in the *Sun*.'

NAFF GOODIES

Tim Brooke-Taylor (see *Naff Old Wykehamists*)
Bill Oddie

NAFF GUESTS ON THE MORECAMBE AND WISE SHOW

Peter Cushing

Hannah Gordon

Glenda Jackson

Harold Wilson

Angela Rippon

Robert Hardy

Judi Dench

Suzanne Danielle

28
GOOD OLD PARKY

CANDIDATES FOR THE ALL-TIME NAFFEST PARKINSON SHOW

INCOHERENT SPORTING EGOMANIACS

Geoffrey Boycott
Brian Clough
F. S. Trueman
Malcolm Allison
Brian Close

ACTRESSES WITH MINDS OF THEIR OWN
(who then tell self-conscious and smutty anecdotes)

Diana Rigg
Joanna Lumley
Susan Hampshire
Glenda Jackson
Maria Aitken
Diana Quick
Helen Mirren

UTTERLY MAD ACTORS
(to put Parky in a good light)

Oliver Reed
Richard Burton
Peter O'Toole
Richard Harris

BORING RACONTEURS

Peter Ustinov
David Niven
Donald Sinden

POPULAR ACADEMIC DROPPING CULTURAL DRAWERS

Desmond Morris
David Attenborough
Jonathan Miller
Kenneth Galbraith
Edward de Bono

INGENUES (for Parky to grope verbally)

Sylvie Kristel
Pia Zadora
Jodie Foster
Stephanie La Motta
Koo Stark

IDIOTS (puffing bestseller)

Shirley Conran
Leslie Thomas
Loony American hag with new diet

HOLLYWOOD ALL-TIME GREATS (affording Parky opportunity to grovel)

Fred Astaire
Bob Hope
Gene Kelly
James Stewart

GHASTLY OLD TROUTS (with minds of their own)

Shirley MacLaine
Marlene Dietrich
Lee Remick
Betty Bacall

MISCELLANEOUS SHOW-OFFS

Lord Porchester
Max Boyce
The priest from Liverpool who pedals round his parish
on a bicycle and holds that Christ would have made a
great stand-up comic
The boring schoolmaster from Liverpool

29
THE FRONT
PAGE

NAFF NEWSPAPERS

The Times (since Harold Evans left)

The *Daily Mail* – the choice of paranoid suburban voyeurs, waddling like Strasbourg geese behind their privet hedges, force-fed on a diet of Lee-Potter, prejudice and fear. (Paradoxically, not the *Sun, Star* or *Daily Express* which are too ridiculous to be naff, though the *Express* is showing signs that it is taking itself seriously and thus might become naff).

The *People*
The *News Of The World*
The *Mail On Sunday*
The *Sunday Express*

NAFF HEADLINES

Thaw Blimey!
Up Your Junta!
Wot A Di!
Bastards!
Gotcha!
The Bravest Women In The Land . . . Lynda Lee-Potter talks to the widows of the Falklands Heroes
The Church And The Bomb – Bel Mooney: A Mother's View
It's Clough Justice!
Now Is The Winter Of Our Di's Content!
A Day Of Shame For Rugby

NAFF PAPERS TO WRITE TO

It's naff to write to any paper except *The Times*. It is extremely naff, however, to write humorous letters to *The Times*, especially in Latin.

Sir,
  Quis custodiet? I note that President Carter's haemmorhoids were recently treated by a Surgeon Rear-Admiral. Fortunate indeed that the good doctor in question was not a Vice-Admiral.
  I remain etc . . .'

Naff By-Line Puffs

Man O'The People
The Woman Columnist Men Can't Ignore
The Man They Can't Gag
The Voice Of Sport
The Man Who Knows The Stars (see David Lewin)
The First Lady Of Fleet Street
The Column With The Sunday Punch
The Man Who's Seen It All Before
The Woman Who Knows The Royals

Naff Journalists

NAFF EDITORS

Sir David English
Sir John Junor
Deirdre McSharry

NAFF COLUMNISTS

Linda Lee-Potter
Jean Rook
George Gale
The Old Codgers
Andrew Alexander (paradoxically not Peregrine
Worsthorne and Auberon Waugh, who only
do it to be irritating)
Ronald Butt
Bernard Levin
Kenneth Rose

NAFF HACKS

Geoffrey Wheatcroft
Richard West
Max Hastings
Celia Brayfield
Mary Kenny
Catherine Olsen
Benny Green

Wilfred De'Ath
Bel Mooney
Patrick Cosgrave
Jilly Cooper

NAFF OCCASIONAL GUEST COLUMNISTS

Larry Adler
Marcia Falkender
Taki
Robert Morley
Clement Freud
Simon Courtauld
Lord Chalfont
Janet Street-Porter
Joanna Lumley
Sharron Davies

NAFF GOSSIP COLUMNISTS

All gossip columnists are naff except William Hickey. Nigel Dempster is super-naff because he alone believes in accuracy.

NAFF TV CRITICS

All TV critics are naff except Julian Barnes, Philip Purser, Russell Davies and William Boyd, but especially naff are:

Margaret Forward
Richard Ingrams
Mary Kenny

NAFF AMERICAN CORRESPONDENTS

Dermot Purgavie
Peter McKay

NAFF INVESTIGATIVE REPORTERS

Trevor Kempson
Ron Mount
Tina Dalgliesh (see *Naff Supergrasses*)
Jon Pilger

NAFF LITERARY EDITORS

Graham Lord
Peter Grosvenor
Philip Howard (see *Naff Metropolitan Critics*)

NAFF THEATRE CRITICS
Milton Shulman
Jack Tinker
John Barber

NAFF SHOW-BIZ CORRESPONDENTS
David Lewin
Donald Zec
Hilary Bonner
Ivan Waterman
Roderick Mann

NAFF SPORTS WRITERS
Laurie Pignon
David Miller
Tommo – The Voice of Sport
Jeff Powell
Ken Jones
Peter West

NAFF AGONY AUNTS
All agony aunts are naff, esp. Claire Rayner and Irma
Kurtz (see *Naff Philosophical Theories*).

NAFF DIMBLEBYS
Bel Mooney

NAFF LEE-POTTERISMS

Look, love . . .

Come off it, love . . .

You didn't shock us, Pam, love, you merely bored us

'I've been entranced by Lena Zavaroni since she was an
eight-year-old belting out "He's Making Eyes At Me".
She's a great star, a formidable talent and a lovely teena-
ger. And in her fight for health and the happiness she's
endlessly given to millions, all I can say is this: "You've
got a nation behind you, love, willing you to succeed."'

NAFF METROPOLITAN CRITICS

All metropolitan critics are naff except John Gross.
Only critics holding academic teaching posts should be
taken seriously.

NAFF THINGS METROPOLITAN CRITICS SAY

'The excellence of the prose is an ample substitute for
positive moral values'

'Anyone in a light-hearted mood can toss off a tragedy;
writing a comedy is far harder'

'There is a level of seriousness that only those capable of
humour can reach'

'Let's hope the so-called intellectual reviewers don't try
and persuade Dick Francis to write a serious
Booker-type novel; he's far too good for that'

'Let's us hope that lesser novelists will follow Kingsley
Amis's example and withdraw their ghastly typescripts
from their publishers so that we can all return to reading
Wodehouse and Waugh'

'Is readability a sin and does it preclude scholarship? No.
Academics seem to feel obliged to be stuffy. We must
also give thanks for *The 27th Kingdom* by Alice Thomas
Ellis. Who said women have no sense of humour?
Finally, Michael Foot's *Debts of Honour*. Terrific stuff. I
never knew the old buzzard could write so well'

'If memory serves . . .'

'Surely it was Flaubert who had it that . . .'

'Flicking idly through the Immortal Sam's *The Lives Of
The Poets* one wet afternoon last week I was struck for
the umpteenth time . . .'

'What a shame Dr Leavis never learned to write
English!'

NAFF FAMILIARITIES

The Divine Songbird
The Immortal Sam
Jane
Sarah
The Master
Old Ovid
'Jamie' Hamilton
'Bertie' Russell
Groucho
Bogart
One Wolfgang Amadeus Mozart
The Immortal Frank Sewards Trueman
Francis Albert Sinatra
Ol' Blue Eyes
St Mugg

NAFF LITERARY QUIZZES

All literary quizzes are naff, esp. those set by Godfrey
Smith
'What colour socks did Martin Chuzzlewit wear?'
'Which of old Chaucer's locquacious pilgrims would
have made the most agreeable companion on an eating
holiday in the Dordogne?'

NAFF GODFREY SMITH
COLLOQUIALISMS

I dunno
Me old mate
A bottle of golden fizz
Jilly Cooper the scrumptious scrivener
Let's be having you!

NAFF AGONY AUNT REMARKS

Women must learn to articulate their needs in bed

Jumping into bed with the first person who comes along is never the answer

To cheat on yourself is the worst betrayal

Don't worry, love. You may be only 32A, but remember this: it's the person behind the tits who does the living (see *Naff Philosophical Theories*)

Not to listen is to invalidate the other person

Sex in the absence of intimacy and tenderness and loving communion reduces the other person to the status of mere object. To offer the body but withhold the soul is a way of expressing underlying anger. Maturity consists in knowing where the body ends and the immortal soul begins (see *Naff Philosophical Theories*)

NAFF NAMES FOR SOCIOLOGY STUDENTS AND POLYTECHNIC TEACHERS IN A COMICAL COLUMN

Ken Turd
Bob Thick
Len Spart
Les Behan

NAFF THINGS JOURNALISTS DO

Exclusively reveal
Visit far-flung trouble-spots
File on-the-spot reports
Indulge in cheque-book journalism (see Sir David English and *Naff Excuses*)

<u>NAFF THINGS JOURNALISTS DO</u>

Write naff obituaries of dead hostesses. Philip Howard writes:

'None knew better than Ann Fleming how to attract intelligent and interesting people to her drawing-room, how to provide them with good food and drink, how to bring light to life, and how to stir the conversational pot and keep it bubbling. She realised the pleasure and value which would come from a table around which civilised people from different walks of life could meet and discuss ideas, politics, literature and gossip. It might be said of her that she elevated gossip to an art and used it for the pleasure of her friends and the enrichment of society. In a world in which high standards are fast disappearing, she provided a welcome oasis of civilised values.'

Write naff obituaries of one another. Geoffrey Wheatcroft writes:

'Philip Hope-Wallace was not a critic – it was not for him to tell composers how to write music – nor one of those who gave that amorphous concept "criticism" a bad name. Philip was an elegant miniaturist, the last English essayist, a journalist who possessed three essential attributes for the part: style, a faultless ear and – rarest of all – a way with an anecdote. For my part I regret that he never wrote his memoirs which might have combined his literary felicity with the saltiness and fun of his conversation. "Are you a wine-bibber?" was the first question he ever put to me. We were on our way by train to the opening night of the Stratford season and the tone of voice suggested that a negative response would bring instant excommunication. So we drank Château Palmer 1956. Just how long ago that was can be gauged not only from the vintage but by the fact that the dining-car was victualled by someone with the wit to know that even in an off year some properties managed to make a very respectable wine. Wine delighted Philip, white, red, pink or, best of all, with bubbles. Yet he rarely wrote about it, I don't know why.'

NAFF JOURNALISTIC EXPRESSIONS

I can exclusively reveal . . . (see *Naff Gossip Columnists*)
Self-appointed
Mother-of-five
So-called expert

Pseudo-intellectual
Woolly-minded liberal
Do-gooder
Innocent women and children
Cowardly bullies
The trendy left
Unrepresentative activists
Rent-a-mob
Naked aggression
Ordinary mother
Joe Average
The taxpayer – that's you and me
Kith and kin
In the final analysis
Light-hearted
Tongue-in-cheek
Irreverent spoof
The compassion lobby
Bomb outrage
Unsung hero

THE NAFFEST ADVERTISEMENT FOR THE *NEW STATESMAN*

Colin Welland writes:
'I'm a very emotional thinker. And when I need to sort myself out – arm myself with good sound arguments – the *Statesman* provides my spear, my arrows. It's the chariot for my fire'

NAFF *SUN* PAGE 3 GIRLS

Denise Perry
Rosalind Runcie

NAFF REMARKS BY PEREGRINE WORSTHORNE

'Better an unequal society that has grown out of British history than an equal society which exists only in the imagination of the so-called intelligentsia of the *Guardian*-reading sort'

'The class system *is* Great Britain, as much as are the White Cliffs of Dover or the changing of the guard outside Buckingham Palace'

'So-called intellectuals fail to grasp that humble people accept wealth and privilege far more readily than they accept coloured immigration because wealth and privilege are part of the British heritage in a way that coloured immigrants are not. Everyone likes a Lord. But nobody likes a coloured neighbour, however cheery and well-mannered.'

'It should be obvious, except perhaps to a *Guardian* reader, that Peter Reeve, the escaped Broadmoor killer, will be more dangerous to the public, rather than less, as a result of having studied sociology at the Open University'

'The most vital social service any government owes its people is not education, or pensions, or medicine, or even justice, but the maintenance of the Queen's peace'

'Without religious sanctions what is to stop people behaving in any way they choose?' (see *Naff Philosophical Theories*)

NAFFEST EDITORIALS OF THE YEAR
(including all in the *Daily Mail* during the Falklands War)

Deirdre McSharry writes:
'"Some of us have become the men we wanted to marry." Trust the gorgeous Gloria Steinem, America's most visible feminist and editor of *MS* magazine, to sock it to us. Summoned to New York for a jolly international seminar of *Cosmo* editors we were agog and ready to learn. Gloria glowed. "Women have achieved a global consciousness-raising. We have the power to choose when we have children. We are redefining work. We are

searching for true sensuality and spirituality. We are against low pay. Against war. Against pornography and violence. Women have a new strategy in politics – called the Gender Gap – and while Reagan holds the White House, women have the country." That's the stuff to give the troops! Then writer Erica Jong took up the banner. "American women have liberated themselves into doing everything. We are entitled to work; entitled to sexual pleasure. I'm a dynamite mother and a good writer. The issue is that we are strong and love ourselves and are proud to be women."

After this rousing start, the conference went with a swing. We editors discovered that work was the preoccupation of our readers whether they live in Amsterdam, Rio or Paris. But to prove that *Cosmo* people know how to play as well as work, that's Brian Braithwaite, our ebullient publisher, and myself above (see *Naff Pictures*) dancing at one of the snazzy parties thrown by Pat Miller, English director of the nineteen international editions. All thanks to Pat and to Helen Gurley Brown, editor-in-chief – and the niftiest dancer on any floor! – for making us feel like honorary New Yorkers.

Meanwhile back in our cosy London office I am glad to welcome Kathleen Jonah, a red-haired American, as new health and beauty editor. "A sense of well-being is addictive", says Kathy, who takes a daily stretch class, sauna and shower before work. *Cosmo*'s shape-up plan and body workshop day (page 54) are specially plotted by Kathy for all mid-winter sloths. Posy Simmonds, our favourite cartoonist, raises our comedy-consciousness with a regular series that starts on page 143. It's the New Year, so tell us what's new and important to you. Bubbly for the best letter.'

Claire Rayner writes:

'Dear MUM

The editor of the *Sunday Mirror* has given me a Christmas treat – this very special place in the paper in which to offer you the *Sunday Mirror*'s good wishes for Christmas.

And also our admiration, gratitude and respect for all you do to keep family life what it has always been in these islands of ours – the cornerstone of everyone's happiness.

He has given it to me, I think, because you and I share so much. I, too, am building up to a crescendo of frantic business.

Like you I worry about getting the shopping done; *Cleaning* the house (in time for everyone to mess it up again!);

Organizing the tree;

Making sure I've got presents for everyone who'll be coming to our house on Christmas Day (will the What-

NAFFEST EDITORIALS OF THE YEAR

sits be bringing their elderly Dad with them? Better get something just in case . . .);

Worrying about everyone's health and comfort;

And *praying* my feet will last out until Boxing Day.

But I'm a great deal more fortunate than many of you. I and my husband have jobs. Our income is enough to stretch to tinsel and turkey and toys for us all.

I'm proud to be one of you, albeit a privileged one. I send you all my heartiest wishes for a loving, happy, family Christmas and a better new year.

I know the editor and everyone else at the Sunday Mirror feels the same.

Yours ever, Claire Rayner'

NAFF MAGAZINES

Options
Health and Efficiency
The Salisbury Review
Titbits
Mayfair
Women's Realm
Radio Times
Cosmopolitan
The *Sunday Express* colour supplement

NAFF MAGAZINE TESTS

Is Your Fella a Wimp?
How Liberated Are You?
What's Your Self-Assertiveness Quotient?
Have You A Sense Of Humour?
Have You Got What It Takes To Be A Successful Hostess?
Does Your Bloke Do His Share Of The Parenting?
Are You A Slut?

NAFF FILM BUFFS

Philip Jenkinson
Sheridan Morley
Barry Norman
Michael Parkinson

NAFF JAZZ BUFFS

All jazz buffs, except professional musicians, are naff,
but Kingsley Amis is especially naff

NAFF HUMOROUS WRITERS

All humorous writers are naff except Auberon Waugh
(and he's naff except in *Private Eye*)

NAFF AUBERON WAUGH COLUMNS

The *Daily Mail*
The *Sunday Telegraph*
The *Spectator*
The *Tatler*
Lancet

THE ALL-TIME NAFFEST
AUBERON WAUGH COLUMN

'The Chief Scout is threatened with losing the £62,000
grant which the Scouts receive from ILEA's Further
Education Committee. Mr Neil Fletcher, its left-wing
chairman, is quoted as saying that he wants to see the
Scouts evolve into a "more socially aware and relevant
organisation".

I suggest that Scouts try a little camouflage. While
getting on with their fieldcraft and country codes, they
should have a look-out posted. As soon as a member of

THE ALL–TIME NAFFEST AUBERON WAUGH COLUMN

ILEA's Further Education Committee is sighted, they should put on scruffy jeans and Gay Liberation T-shirts and start shouting left-wing slogans and random obscenities.

Once a year they might hold a sort of General Inspection in reverse, making their Scout hut as dirty as possible for inspection by the Further Education Committee, who would find them lounging around smoking pot and watching Channel 4 on television.'

NAFF OLD *PRIVATE EYE* JOKES

Geddit!
Shome mishtake here shurely
Ugandan discussions
Ongoing legover situation
I think we should be told
See P 94
Richard Ingrams
For it is he

NAFF NEW *PRIVATE EYE* JOKES

The Private Eye Story – The First Twenty-one Years (see *Naff Cover-ups*)

─30─
THE ROYALS

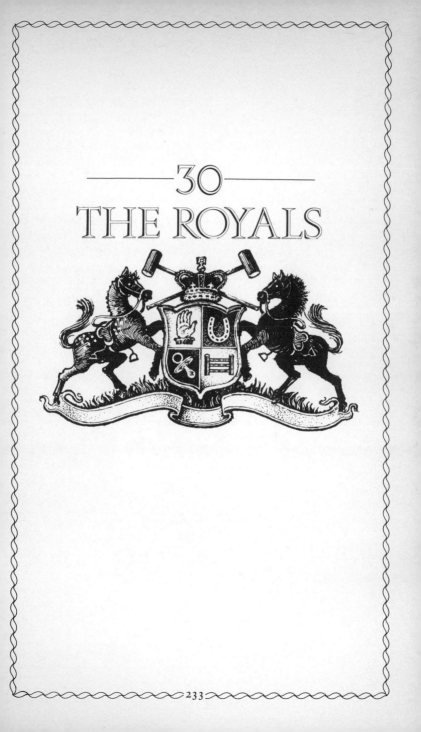

NAFF THINGS PEOPLE SAY
ABOUT ROYALTY

Grace Kelly was a princess from the moment she was born

The Queen is so poor she has to spend her own money

The Royals go to the toilet too, you know

Mark Phillips has a mortgage

Princess Anne is actually a nice person in an impossible situation

'Yes – even a princess can get those baby blues . . .' (Clare Dover, Medical Correspondent of the *Daily Express*)

'When Mrs Sarah Jones, widow of the Falklands Hero Colonel H, accepted his VC, what the Queen said to her meant more to her than the medal itself.' The *Daily Express*

'When a member of the Royal Family turns up late for a major Royal occasion being graced by the Queen herself questions are bound to be asked.' The *Daily Mirror*

Billy Marsh, the man who books the stars, writes: 'Showbiz stars will drop everything to appear in the Royal Variety Performance. Even legendary American entertainers like Howard Keel and Rosmary Clooney put the chance of meeting our first family above all else. When I asked Howard Keel to take part in this year's show at London's Drury Lane Theatre, it meant choosing between TV nasty J. R. Ewing and the Queen Mum. Howard didn't hesitate. He told me: "Don't worry, Billy, it's no contest. I'll be on that plane to London".'

Nigel Dempster writes:
'The heir to the throne came in for some gentle ribbing yesterday when the Queen met staff on the occasion of the Foreign Office's two-hundredth anniversary. Communications official John Brown told her: "Perhaps you could have a word with Prince Charles – he is rather notorious for losing or failing to return Despatch Boxes." Clearly in on the joke – Charles is a notoriously slow reader when it comes to official papers – Her Majesty, roaring with laughter, replied: "Why don't you tell him yourself!"'

Jean Rook, writes:
For a split second a whole choked nation held the breath for which The Queen Mum was fighting. This morning we breathe again.

NAFF THINGS PEOPLE SAY ABOUT ROYALTY

Not least those of us in Fleet Street who, had that fishbone gone too deep, would in the smallest darkest hours of our working lives have had to dash off hundreds of words with our tears. The Queen Mum is eighty-two and the facts of her life are always to the hands which would rush them to the front-page when, God forbid, she loses it. But our true feelings are unwritten as the man in the street's are unspoken.

As it is, dear Ma'am, you've thankfully left me nothing to say which hasn't been better said by the Clarence House Spokesman who delightedly told the breath-holding world: "We understand she will soon be back with us".'

NAFF THINGS THE ROYAL FAMILY DO

Walkabouts
Visit disaster victims (as if they didn't have enough to worry about already)
Live in a fish-bowl
Fail to answer back
Slaughter wildlife
Windsurf
Display a Goonish sense of humour
Go to university with three 'O' levels
Have slight chills
Have more than one birthday

NAFF ROYAL BUM-SUCKERS

Godfrey Talbot
Ivor Herbert
Lady Antonia Fraser
Gordon Honeycombe
Anthony Holden
Hugh Montgomery-Massingberd
Lady Elizabeth Longford
Nigel Dempster
Penny Junor
Robert Lacey

31
THE WORLD OF BOOKS

NAFF PUBLISHERS

Souvenir Press
Paul Hamlyn
Hodder and Stoughton
New English Library
Pavilion Books
Arrow Books
W. H. Allen
Robert Hale

NAFF THINGS PUBLISHERS SAY TO AUTHORS

'The ending's not quite right . . .'
'*I* loved it, but I'm afraid they'll never understand it in America . . .'
'I'll be in Frankfurt . . .'
'I'm on the other line . . .'
'Hullo Simon – sorry – *Stephen*, of *course*, I . . .'
'The cheque's been signed and we're waiting for . . .'
'I loved the duck.'
'*I* liked it, but the Sales Director's wife thought . . .'
'Yes, but will it sell in Warrington?'
'It just needs a bit of tightening.'
'This calls for the old blue pencil.'

NAFF THINGS AUTHORS SAY TO PUBLISHERS

'Couldn't you read it over Christmas?'
'All editors are frustrated writers at heart.'
'I may not be Tolstoy but I can tell a rattling good yarn.'
'It made my typist *roar* with laughter.'
'Does it matter if I've given the nymphomaniac drug-addict the name of my first wife?'
'I suppose you'll want a photograph for the cover.'

NAFF THINGS AUTHORS SAY TO PUBLISHERS

'Don't worry about me. I just wrote the bloody thing.'
'You mean bookshops can send them back?'
'Excuse the spelling.'
'I see Gore Vidal was on "The South Bank Show" last night. Perhaps you could have a quiet word with that nice PR girl.'
'My mother couldn't find a copy in her local bookshop. And if *they* can't get a copy . . .'

NAFF DEDICATIONS AND ACKNOWLEDGEMENTS

To my parents without whom . . .
To my wife without whom . . .
To Clive James for helping me with the grammar
To Gore Vidal for the use of his house
To the admirable Miss Casparry for typing the manuscript (and managing to decipher my abominable writing!)

The inexhaustible patience and unfailing encouragement of my publisher, Tom Maschler, and my literary agent, Graham Watson are, to put it mildly, a great deal more than I deserve. Brian Inglis kindly read the proofs; this action was the fruit of a pact he and I made many years ago, by the terms of which we pledged ourselves always to proof-read each other's books. Since then, however, he has published nine and this is only my second; *sunt lacrimae rerum*. Finally I have to thank that unseen and many-headed friend, my readers.

While wishing to acknowledge all the help I've received on this book I must emphasise that the mistakes are mine and mine alone. (Very naff. If the author recognised the mistakes as his, why didn't he change them? And if he didn't recognise them as mistakes, how does he know they are his?)

NAFF SPEAKERS AT A FOYLES LUNCH

Richard Baker
Robert Morley
Malcolm Muggeridge
John Mortimer
Lady Antonia Fraser
Margaret Powell
Richard Gordon
Angela Rippon
Bernard Miles
Nanette Newman
Michael Parkinson

NAFF SHELVES IN A BOOKSHOP

Psychology
Astrology
Sex and Health
Humour
Philosophy (at Hatchards)

NAFF BESTSELLERS OF 1984

Malcolm Muggeridge: A Life, by Christopher Booker
Flower-Pressing Was For Sundays: Some Childhood Weekends by Dirk Bogarde
Pop Stars' Number Twos, by Paula Yates
Kenneth Williams's Book of Literary Ripostes
Joanna Lumley's 1982 Diary – collected from *The Times*
Chocks Away, Gentlemen Please! Vol. II of Sir John Mills's autobiography
We Are Not Amused! – hilarious royal mishaps, collated by Angela Rippon
Elizabeth Windsor: Mother, by Bel Mooney
Coo-ee! Further Musings From The Sage Of Myrtlebank, Arthur Marshall

NAFF BESTSELLERS OF 1984

Encore Un Rip-Off – Miles Kington, another collection
of *Franglais*

NAFF BLURBS

'A funny, irreverent novel which could serve as a primer
on how to make a classy stag-film, *Blue Movie* is not for
the squeamish. Anyone who expects it to be another of
Terry Southern's zany, kinky, tongue-in-cheek pieces of
naughtiness will not be disappointed!'
                              Panther

32
WAXING
PHILOSOPHICAL

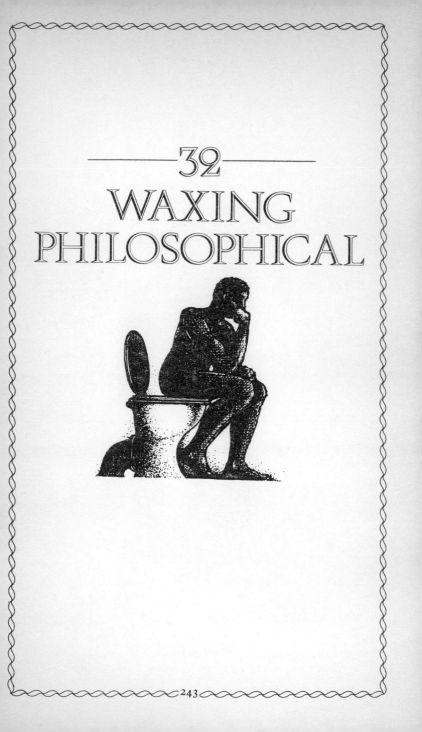

NAFF PHILOSOPHERS

NAFF REAL PHILOSOPHERS

Anthony Quinton. A nine-to-five philosopher who spends too much time answering the naff questions of plain men on naff radio programmes such as 'Any Questions' and who should be ashamed of himself for accepting a peerage from Mrs Thatcher.

NAFF SNUG-BAR PHILOSOPHERS

Peter Allis
Tom Crabtree
Bob Topping
Quincy

NAFF SALOON BAR PHILOSOPHERS

Richard West
Jeffrey Bernard
Hilda Ogden
Fred Trueman

NAFF EL VINO'S PHILOSOPHERS

Alan Watkins
Geoffrey Wheatcroft
George Gale

NAFF WINE BAR PHILOSOPHERS

Quentin Crisp

NAFF POLITICAL PHILOSOPHERS

Enoch Powell
Tom's Uncle Arthur

NAFF CLUB PHILOSOPHERS

Lord Hailsham
General Sir John Hackett

NAFF WOMEN'S INSTITUTE PHILOSOPHERS

Mary Kenny
Arthur Marshall

NAFF AGREEABLE COUNTRY CHURCHYARD PHILOSOPHERS

Malcolm Muggeridge
Christopher Booker
Jack Hargreaves

NAFF WISE OLD BIRD PHILOSOPHERS

William Deedes
James Cameron
Ted Moult
John Arlott
Rene Cutforth

NAFF HIGH-TABLE THEOLOGIANS

Dr Edward Norman

NAFF THINGS DR EDWARD NORMAN SAYS

'Nuclear weapons are a sort of black joke by the good Lord God, a reminder that the author of the creation is still in charge, however much trendy theologians may prate away about the autonomy of man.' (See *Naff Philosophical Theories*)

NAFF PHILOSOPHICAL THEORIES

Moral relativism. One shouldn't interfere with the internal arrangements of a foreign society. There is no logical difficulty in attaching a non-relative morality of toleration or non-interference to a view of morality as relative. When in Rome . . .

The truth, as always, lies somewhere in the middle. To suggest that if the truth really were, as this excellent principle requires, half way between A and Z, for all values of A and Z, then it must also be half way between the half way point between A and Z and Z and so on *ad infinitum*, is merely frivolous.

It's the girl behind the tits that does the living (see *Naff Things Agony Aunts Say*)

Vitalism. A life principle pulses through the universe.

Fatalism. If the statement 'I will be run over by a bus' is

true it's true now, if false, false now. Therefore there is no point in looking to left and right before crossing the road.

Waltzing is not the same thing as dancing, since the rhumba is also a dance but it is not a waltz. It therefore follows that one can waltz without dancing the waltz.

Absolute Idealism. There is no truth short of the whole. Even a proposition such as 'this is a table' is false just as far as it is abstract. We are all moments in the mind of a self-thinking thought.

Ontological collectivism. The nation is more real than its individual members. The proof of this is that the attributes of a group cannot necessarily be predicated of its members. Thus, the Japanese nation is larger than the Swedish nation, but, on the whole, cheery Japanese gentlemen are smaller than individual Swedes.

Ethical collectivism. The common good of the nation is not simply the sum of the interests of its members. The welfare of the nation is not the aggregate of individual welfares.

Just as a pair of shoes is three things – the left shoe, the right shoe and the pair – so is a nation at least two things: the class of all its attributes and itself.

Nationalism is an inherited characteristic.

Without constraints on freedom of speech there could be no such thing as freedom of speech.

You can't legislate against human nature.

Something possible in a thousand years will become inevitable in a billion.

The Argument from Morality. Morality requires and presupposes religion. Value is not part of the world. But we know there is value. Therefore God must have put it there.

Optimism. Despite appearances, this world is the best of all possible worlds. All the evil in the world is the price that has to be paid for a greater good – the existence of free-will. Indeed, the work most worthy of God involves the eternal damnation of the majority of men.

NAFF PHILOSOPHICAL THEORIES

To owe allegiance to the crown and to be born in the United Kingdom as a citizen of the place are the same thing.

There's no such thing as a free lunch.

We are all Falklanders now.

NAFF TAUTOLOGIES

'The theory of evolution's only a theory, you know'

NAFF NON-SCIENTIFIC THEORIES

Astrology
Creationism
Marxism
Women's intuition
God's mysterious ways
The F-Plan diet

33
THE
INTERNATIONAL
SCENE

LA GRANDE NAFFE

EUROPEANS

Mireille Mathieu
Karl-Heinz Rummeniger
Sacha Distel
Prince Rainier
Philippe Junot
The Dutch Royal family
Demis Roussos
Arianna Stassinopoulous
Egon Ronay
Giscard d'Estaing
The Gnomes of Zurich
Carlo Ponti
Nana Mouskouri
Simone Signoret
Nathalie Delon
The Duchess of Bedford
Emil Zatopek
Zizi Jeanmaire
Didier Millinaire
Olga Korbut
Melina Mercouri
Dino de Laurentiis
The Spanish football team
Taki
Serge Gainsbourg
Maurice Chevalier
Juliette Greco
Regine
Richard Clayderman (esp. if referred to as
Monsieur Music)

AMERICAN

Lee Marvin
Martha 'the Mouth' Mitchell
President Nixon
Telly Savalas
Senator Edward Kennedy
Sammy Davis Jr
E.T.

AMERICAN

Helen Gurley Brown
Lassie
Mark McCormack
The Moral Majority cow
Dr Spock
Mr Spock
Captain Kirk
Charles 'Chuck' Colson
John Dean
Gordon Liddy
William F. Buckley
Betty Bacall
John Irving
Paul Anka
Shirley MacLaine
Liza Minelli
Hugh Hefner
Spiro Agnew
Robert Carrier
Victor Kiam

THE REST

Ossie Ardiles
Trini Lopez
Little Doc
Ian Smith
Malcolm Fraser
Xavier Cugat
Richie Benaud
El Loco (Peruvian goalkeeper)
Ricardo Montalban
Carmen Miranda
Kerry Packer
Ephrem Zimbalist Jr
Emperor Bokassa
Julio Iglesias
Sheikh Yamani
Bianca Jagger
Rolf Harris
Carmen Callil
Lady Tryon
Chips Rafferty

34
A GAZE INTO THE CRYSTAL BALL

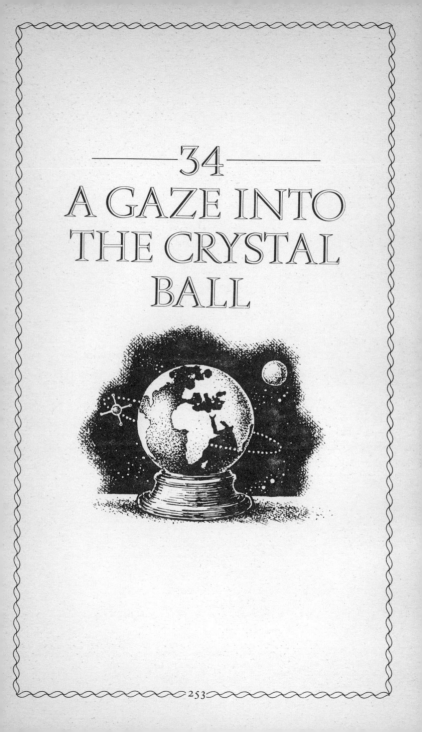

NAFF PREDICTIONS FOR 1984

Sir John Mills receives an Oscar for general attitude.

Sir David English becomes editor of the *The Times*. Paul Johnson writes: 'So-called intellectuals may sneer, but Sir David understands Fleet Street.'

Sir David English commissions nine new episodes of *We'll Meet Again*. The senior features writer resigns and is replaced by Jilly Cooper. Paul Johnson writes: 'So-called intellectuals may sneer, but Jilly Cooper knows what her readers want.'

Sir A. J. Ayer appears on 'The Paula Yates Show'.

Princess Margaret holidays in Mustique with John Inman.

Mark Thatcher does a TV commercial for tinned turkey. Sebastian Coe becomes a born again Christian.

The National Theatre takes over the Prince of Wales Theatre for a season of William Douglas-Home plays. Paul Johnson writes: 'So-called intellectuals may sneer, but Douglas-Home is a master of the well-made play'.

Kingsley Amis writes a series of articles for the *Sunday Telegraph* attacking the pinko conspiracy at the BBC.

Anthony Howard becomes editor of the *Observer*.

A film about an alien child dying of bone cancer grosses £5 million a day. Sir David English buys the publication rights for *The Times*. Paul Johnson writes: 'The fashionable *avant-garde* may sneer but I found the film very touching'.

Kingsley Amis accuses 'Panorama' of being an extension of the Soviet propaganda service.

Five senior BBC producers turn up in Moscow wearing cocktail dresses. Paul Johnson isn't surprised.

Paul Johnson becomes a life peer.

Prince Andrew announces his engagement to a pudding-faced royal eventer from Lichtenstein.

Lawrie McMenemy and Colonel H's widow join Mrs Thatcher's cocktail cabinet. Paul Johnson writes: 'Trendy liberals may sneer, but I'd trust Mrs Thatcher's gut instinct for what the public wants.'

Nigel Dempster sues Harold Pinter for libel.

On television, Richard Ingrams denies that there is any inconsistency in Nigel Dempster's action. 'People in the

NAFF PREDICTIONS FOR 1984

public eye like Pinter must expect to be sued for libel.'

The Royals defeat the Grapplers in the televised final of Pro/Celebrity wrestling.

Michael Meacher says that the market economy is a form of censorship.

In the course of a charity football match at Wembley, Glasgow Rangers supporters invade the pitch and kill Sir Stanley Matthews.

Jane Fonda becomes a senator.

Little and Large appear as Bottom and Quince in the National Theatre's production of *A Midsummer Night's Dream*.

Sir Kenneth Newman appears on 'The Morecambe and Wise Show'.

Michael Meacher complains that the average working man has as much chance of being asked to write a leading article for *The Times* as a Moscow peasant has of getting his views aired in *Pravda*. Paul Johnson ripostes by pointing out that there's more class consciousness in the Kremlin than ever you'll find on a rainy afternoon in White's.

In a tragic case of mistaken identity, the police shoot a peace demonstrator's ex-girlfriend's mother-in-law's sister, who was once a go-go dancer. Alan Clark MP says: 'For the police to do such a thing she must have been tainted with criminality.' Lynda Lee-Potter writes: 'This is what you must expect if you dance topless.' Eldon Griffiths MP says that the blame lies squarely with Parliament for voting against the noose. The *Sunday Telegraph* blames soft sentencing and the permissive climate and Sir Kenneth Newman, while of course regretting the incident, points out that it highlights the risks the ordinary bobby on the beat runs these days.

Norman Tebbit becomes Home Secretary.

Jimmy Savile receives a knighthood.

Clare Francis becomes a Dame of the British Empire.

The Rolling Stones give a concert in aid of Help The Aged

Elton John stands for parliament as an SDP candidate.

Desmond Wilcox is appointed head of Channel 4.